# MRS. WITTY'S
# MONSTER
# COOKIES

## by Helen Witty

## Illustrations by
## Tedd Arnold

Workman Publishing,
New York

# DEDICATION

To Richard, for good and sufficient reasons.

*Library of Congress Cataloging in Publication Data*

Witty, Helen.
  Mrs. Witty's monster cookies.
  Includes index.
  1. Cookies.   I. Title.
TX772.W55   1983     641.8'654     83-40035
ISBN 0-89480-609-2

Cover and book design: Douglass Grimmett
Cover and book illustrations: Tedd Arnold

Workman Publishing Company, Inc.
1 West 39 Street
New York, NY 10018

Manufactured in the United States of America
First printing October 1983
10  9  8  7  6  5  4  3  2  1

# CONTENTS

## MARVELOUS MEDIUM-SIZE MOUTHFULS

# A Cook's Tale

A little nursery tale tells of a magic pancake so delicious to look at and to smell that everyone who saw or sniffed it—beginning with the cook—wanted to devour it on the spot. This alarmed the pancake; having magical powers, it leapt out of the pan and rolled merrily away, the populace in pursuit.

Now I have a theory that the pancake was the first monster cookie, and the cookie craze that more or less grips the nation today is merely the continuation of that fabled chase. I should admit right here that my memory of the story yields no clue as to whether the fugitive was caught and eaten, so I choose to believe my own happy ending: each pursuer, in turn, peeled off and returned home to confect a personal version of the one that got away. While the cookie rolled gleefully on, cookie recipes were born, and multiplied, and multiplied . . .

Well, it seems likely to me. For what have we here on the gastronomic scene? Veritable cookie madness. Everywhere, in big city and small town, bake-in and take-out shops purvey the rich-rich concoctions of this cookie-pusher or that one. Publicity wars sputter between cookie entrepreneurs who are known, like royalty, by their first names only.

Baking ovens equipped just for cookies are cunningly planted in supermarkets to waft their aromas abroad, to the downfall of dieters. A full-grown restaurant critic complains in print when, in a fancy restaurant, the tray of after-dinner cookies is not offered at her table.

Clearly cookies are *in,* the modern manna for sybarites. They have come into their own after centuries of being called tea cakes, or biscuits, or wafers, or jumbles, or hermits, or snaps. They have climbed out of the cookie jar and started rolling.

About here someone will ask, Why this book? Why is Mrs. Witty probing deeply into cookie lore and devising foolproof cookie formulas if many perfectly edible renderings are available in the world? To honor the pleasure principle, that's why. To strike a blow for monstrous depravity. To lead from the store-bought wilderness those who would like to bake their own bonny and superior sweets when cookie-hunger strikes.

Further, among all those cookies out there, there are all too few Big Moments along the lines of that original cookie I was telling you about. There are far too few killer cookies that can fairly be described as Monsters (6 inches in diameter), much less as Maximonster (9 inches) or Ultimates (12 inches).

Something now has been done about that state of affairs. Among these rec-ipes you will find the big-bigger-biggest ones, plus subcompacts and minimonsters, medium-size pielets and ''pillows''; bar cookies that include brownies in six shades, from platinum to deepest chocolate; middling-large cookies scented with ginger and orange, mincemeat and nuts, cinnamon, vanilla, and almond; chocolate chips crammed into hefty rounds of dough of all sizes, flavored with peanut butter, or chocolate, or coffee, or classic brown sugar. And there's more—the fifty recipes are bakable in around seventy-five versions. Enough to get on with, if you're serious about this.

Back there someplace I mentioned killer cookies. Yes, indeed, these cookies *are* compounded of butter, and brown sugar, and chocolate, and nuts, and a dozen other sumptuous things that fall beyond the pale of a minimalist diet; some of them—let's face it—are loaded. But I want to tell you how I delude myself while testing and tasting: These cookies are *not fattening—*so long as they're eaten standing up!

What that iffy condition, shared with guests, might do to a proper tea party, I'm not sure. (Social advice is beyond the scope of this book.) I just want to pass along the how-to's of making a heap of *good* cookies, from the gaggle of giants described above to dainty nibbles that are indeed suitable for tea parties. Beyond that, you're on your own. You may never need to buy cookies again.

# COOKIECRAFT

Including Equipment, Ingredients, and Techniques.

# EQUIPMENT

This basic list includes all the utensils (and a few supplies) needed to accomplish by hand all of the cookie-baking in this book. If you are using an electric mixer and/or a food processor, be sure you understand their use; consult the manufacturer's manual before beginning.

## BAKING PANS

**Baking sheets** are large, flat pans either without edges or with the ends or all four sides very slightly turned up. It's good to have two of these, even though you'll bake on only one at a time. Baking sheets are available in shiny aluminum (very satisfactory), or with a nonstick coating such as Teflon or Silverstone (also excellent), or they may have been given a special dark glaze or finish that affects both baking times and temperatures. (Such pans as these are best left to professional bakers, unless you like to experiment.) Choose heavyweight baking sheets rather than thin ones, and be sure that those you buy are at least 4 inches shorter and 4 inches narrower than the inside of your oven. Too-large pans block heat circulation and cause uneven baking.

**8-inch square pans** are ideal for baking bar cookies. These pans have sides about 1½ inches high and can be used for cakes, cornbread, and so on, as well as brownies and other bar cookies. Either aluminum or nonstick-coated pans are fine. If you use an ovenproof glass pan, you'll need to reduce the oven temperature by 25°F to prevent overbaking the contents.

**9-inch pie pan.** This will turn out a 7-inch round of shortbread when the dough covers the bottom without touching the sides. Choose an aluminum or nonstick pan. If you use an ovenproof glass pan, the oven temperature must be reduced by 25°F to prevent overbaking. (Another use for either the pie pan or the 8-inch square pan: when you have too few cookies to fill a baking sheet, invert one of the smaller pans and bake the cookies on the bottom. This avoids the problems of baking a few cookies on a large expanse of pan—some are sure to burn, for complicated reasons having to do with heat transfer.)

**12-inch pizza pan.** Only if you have designs for baking Ultimate Cookies (page 38) will you need this, an inexpensive pan measuring 12 inches across, exclusive of the flat rim. These pans are widely sold in supermarkets.

**Foil:** Aluminum foil, both regular and heavy-duty, should be kept on hand. A sheet of foil can stand in for an extra baking sheet, making it possible to bake batches in rapid sequence when you want to get a small production line going. (While the first sheetful is baking, form the next batch of cookies on the foil, greased or not, as directed; when the baking sheet has been completely cooled after removing the cookies, slide the laden foil onto it and bake away.) Regular foil is sometimes used for covering the baking sheet before baking certain delicate cookies. It helps prevent overbaking or actual scorching. Foil is also used to shield the tops of the very large cookies during their long baking.

## MEASURING UTENSILS

**Dry-measuring cups,** usually made of stainless steel or plastic, are best for measuring dry ingredients and such things as brown sugar and shortening because the top of the contents can be leveled to assure exact measurement. They come in nested sets in sizes ranging downward from 1 cup (some sets have a 2-cup measure) through ½ cup, ⅓ cup, and ¼ cup; some sets include a handy ⅛-cup (2-tablespoon) measure.

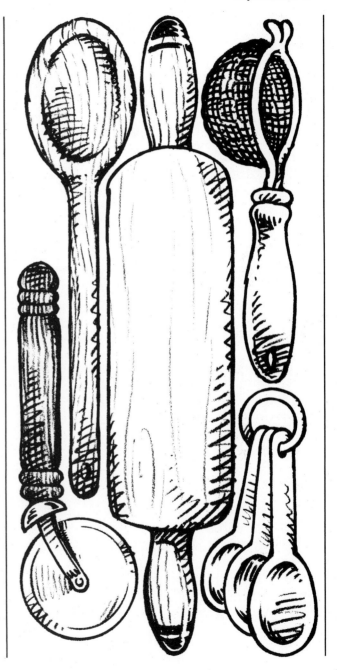

**Liquid-measuring cups,** of glass or plastic, allow easy judging of the level of liquid or semiliquid ingredients. The 1-cup size is adequate for most recipes, but pint and quart measures are useful too.

**Measuring spoons** come in nested sets; they are most often made of stainless steel or plastic. Always use these—spoons intended for table use are not made to precise size standards.

## SIFTERS

**Fine-mesh sieve:** This will do in place of a **flour sifter** if you don't care to invest in that nonessential gadget for mixing dry ingredients and removing lumps from flour, sugar, and the like. (See Techniques, page 19.) Choose a stainless-steel or nylon mesh sieve in preference to one of tinned steel, which rusts easily.

## MIXING AND DOUGH-SHAPING UTENSILS

See Techniques (page 19) for comments on the use of mixing machines. For hand mixing, here's what you need:

**Mixing bowl,** of pottery or stainless steel, holding 3 quarts or more. You'll want a smaller bowl or two for peripheral operations.

**Large mixing spoon,** preferably of wood.

**Whisk:** A 12-inch stainless-steel whisk of narrow, rather than bulbous, shape is good for a variety of jobs. Technically, this is a sauce whisk.

**Rubber spatulas:** Several of these in various sizes are invaluable for mixing and folding, scraping bowls, flattening cookies before baking, and spreading batter in the pan.

**Pastry blender:** This isn't essential; you can use two table knives for cutting solid shortening into a flour mixture (see Techniques, page 19).

**Pastry bag:** This is actually a simple device, not at all scary (see Techniques, page 19, on how to use the pastry bag). They now come in easy-to-clean plastic material and are recommended if you'd like to make especially pretty macaroons or shape a lot of drop cookies in a hurry. Get a large star tube for maca-roons, a large plain tube for drop cook-ies. The alternative for both types of cookies is to drop dough from the tip of a teaspoon.

**Rolling pin:** If you're investing in one of these, get a smooth hardwood pin as large as can be handled comfortably; don't dally with rickety lightweights. Lacking a rolling pin, you can make do with a tall, straight wine bottle.

**Rolling surface:** Use a pastry board or marble slab or Formica countertop, if you have it. But, with the technique recommended (rolling dough between sheets of plastic wrap), you can make do with any smooth, flat surface.

**Pastry wheel** (a cutting wheel with a plain edge) or a **pastry jagger** (this has a "pinked" edge): Either of these quickly and easily cuts strips or any geometrical shapes from rolled-out dough. But a sharp knife will also do the job.

**Cake tester,** or a **thin skewer,** or even a **cocktail pick,** and a **ruler:** Good for checking the thickness of rolled-out dough. Be sure to keep a ruler on hand. I like the 15-inch size and keep one of this length standing in the crock with the whisks and spoons; it is frequently used for checking pan sizes, the diame-ter of rolled-out pastry, and so on.

**Round cookie cutters** are used for pastry and biscuits, too. They are plain-edged or fluted. A 2½-inch cutter and a slightly larger size, 2¾ inches, are suggested.

# BAKING, TESTING, COOLING, AND CUTTING UTENSILS

**Oven thermometer:** Well, yes, most ovens *do* have a thermostat, but unless it is checked frequently by a service-man, chances are that your oven tem-perature is 25 or more degrees off. The remedy is to keep a thermometer in the oven and consult it before you begin baking and before each subsequent batch. Get a mercury thermometer—the all-metal devices that register tempera-tures on a dial are not to be recom-mended, because even a slight fall or a jolt or two can make them permanently unreliable.

**Timer:** A necessity if your range isn't equipped with one. Set it for a shorter time than the minimum suggested for the cookies, then check baking progress at once when it goes off. This will spare you surprises—cookies aren't always done exactly when the recipe says they should be.

**Cake tester** (optional): Doneness of bar cookies is best judged by touch and sight; however, using a cake tester—a short length of stiff wire with a hang-ing loop at one end—is a security blan-ket for some. If the tester emerges clean and dry after being thrust into the center of a panful of brownies (or a cake layer), the batch is done. You can use a thin metal skewer, a wooden cocktail pick, or the nonworking end of a wooden match. Granny used a straw pulled from a new broom and set aside for the purpose.

**Metal spatula:** Either one of the long, narrow, flexible sort, or one with an angled shape (pancake turner) to use for lifting hot cookies to racks and for removing bar cookies from their pan after cooling.

**Wire racks** are essential for cooling cookies; best if large rather than small. Look for sturdy racks, preferably of stainless steel, with wires set closely together.

**Serrated knife:** The most satisfactory type for cutting bar cookies, slicing Fruit Newts (page 120), and so on is a blade with serrations that aren't too coarse. For slicing chilled, molded dough, a very sharp straight knife or a finely serrated knife are equally good.

# Containers and Supplies for Storage

**Canisters,** or traditional **cookie jars,** or **plastic kitchen containers** (with lids), for room-temperature storage, are all fine. For crisp cookies, the covers should be a bit loose, but soft and chewy cookies should be covered tightly. Brownies can be left in their pan (just cover them with foil or plastic wrap).

**Plastic wrap** or **bags** and **aluminum foil** are also convenient to use for refrigerating cookies. If you are freezing cookies, plastic bags should be freezer-weight, and batches wrapped in sheet plastic or foil should be sealed with tape. You can also use tightly covered rigid plastic freezer containers. (See Techniques, page 19, for wrapping methods for very large cookies.)

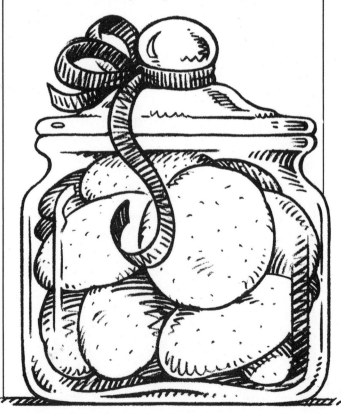

# INGREDIENTS

Manners maketh man, says the poet, but only fine ingredients make wonderful cookies. Some thoughts on what goes into the best.

## FLOURS

**All-purpose flour** ( I prefer it unbleached) is the kind to use for almost all the cookies herein. In addition, some doughs contain a share of cornstarch, or whole-wheat flour, or even cornmeal, but faithful all-purpose flour is the backbone.

To measure flour, see Techniques, page 19.

You'll notice that some recipes call for a small amount of extra liquid to be added if the dough proves to be dry. (Because flours may contain varying amounts of moisture due to atmospheric conditions, it's impossible to be sure that the amount of flour called for is exactly right.) Conversely, if a dough should turn out to be too soft to roll and cut, a little flour can be worked in to improve matters. Such adjustments should be made cautiously, a little liquid or a little flour at a time.

**Cornstarch** is included in some recipes as a stand-in for part of the flour because of the uniquely crisp texture it contributes. For instance, I use it (and prefer it) in shortbread in place of hard-to-find rice flour.

## SHORTENINGS

**Butter** is called for in most of my cookie recipes because its wonderful flavor is important to the result. Further, **unsalted** (''sweet'') **butter** is strongly suggested. Its delicate, creamlike taste is quite unlike that of most salted butters, but if it is not on hand, lightly salted regular butter can be substituted. Unsalted or salted regular **margarine** can also be used; however, whipped margarine, which contains added water, won't do. If salt is an ingredient in the cookie recipe you're contemplating, reduce the quantity by half if you use salted rather than unsalted butter or margarine.

**Vegetable shortening** is specified, in whole or in part, in certain recipes because of its greater ''shortening'' power. It is also called for in recipes for certain cookies that are highly spiced or otherwise flavored with ingredients that would mask the flavor of butter, if it were used.

**Oil** should not be substituted when any solid shortening is specified unless you're prepared to whip out a home economics handbook and calculate the needed recipe changes. But do use a good quality corn oil or other bland oil in the Quick Nutted Brownies on page 86 (the only recipe which calls for oil).

**Measurements:** Butter and margarine are interchangeable, measure for measure. However, if shortening (or lard) is substituted for butter or margarine, the amount used should be reduced by about 20 percent (try that on your pocket calculator). And, in reverse, increase the amount of butter or margarine by about 20 percent when substituting it for shortening or lard. Lard, incidentally, is really important to the Almond Cookies, More or Less Chinese (page 94), if you want them to taste superbly authentic. Consult your own taste about substituting lard for shortening or butter in other recipes.

# EGGS

Standard U.S. ''large'' eggs went into the making of the cookie doughs described in this book. Eggs of this size average 2 ounces in weight, so, if you have small or very large eggs, you can substitute, with the help of a small kitchen scale or a lot of experience. Bear in mind that putting in too much egg (which is, of course, quite liquid) results in a too-soft dough; insufficient egg results in dough that is too dry.

# LEAVENINGS

Some recipes in this book include no leavening at all—no baking powder, no baking soda, not even air incorporated by way of beaten egg whites. This is as it should be and not the result of somnolence on the part of author, editor, proofreader, or anyone else.

# SWEETENERS

Cookie sweeteners include granulated sugar, confectioners' sugar, light and dark brown sugar, honey, molasses, and light and dark corn syrup. In addition, candied fruits, dried fruits, sweetened coconut, and so on also add sweetness to certain cookies. Some sweet talk:

**Granulated sugar** in an ingredient list means regular granulated sugar unless extra-fine (or superfine) or coarse sugar is specified. Very coarse sugar makes an attractive cookie topping—in Big Sugars (page 56), for instance—but regular sugar is fine for decoration, too.

**Confectioners' sugar** or **10X sugar** is best known as **powdered sugar** in some regions. It is much less sweet, measure for measure, than granulated sugar, and it also contains a little cornstarch, added to prevent it from becoming rock-hard. Expectably, it behaves differently from granulated sugar in baked goods, and it shouldn't be substituted unless you're prepared to revise the recipe pretty drastically. Confectioners' sugar is fine in recipes that have been worked out with its particular characteristics in mind; Vanilla Shortbread (page 88) is one example.

**Brown sugar:** When it is called for, either dark or light can be used, although light sugar is preferable for delicate cookies. Dark brown sugar has a slightly molasses-like flavor, especially good as a background for spices. Measure brown sugar by packing it firmly into the cup; it should hold its shape when it's turned out.

**Honey** can't be substituted for dry sweetenings without extensive adjustments, but when the recipe has been written to include it, it adds distinctive flavor. If a delicate honey is called for, don't substitute a dark, strong one, and vice versa.

**Corn syrup,** light or dark, can be substituted for honey, and likewise honey for corn syrup. Light syrup has little or no flavor, whereas dark syrup is reminiscent of molasses, but milder.

# CHOCOLATE

Could there be cookie life without chocolate? It's doubtful. Cookies are enlivened by chocolate in many forms, some more or less sweetened, others not sweetened at all.

**Baking** or **unsweetened chocolate** is melted before it's added to certain doughs. Lacking sugar, it is too stern in flavor to be used as chunks in baked things. Baking chocolate and cocoa are interchangeable only if certain recipe adjustments are made.

**Sweet chocolate,** meaning dark sweet chocolate, has its uses in cookies as well as cakes (and as fodder for candy eaters). The brand name ''German's'' on the label of the best-known packaged brand commemorates the man who developed the formula a century ago.

**Semisweet chocolate,** falling midway between the first two, comes in half-pound bars or packages of individually wrapped squares. It can be melted, or it can be chopped to become chocolate ''chips.'' But it's best known in the shape of specially formulated and bagged **chocolate pieces** (or **bits,** or **morsels,** or **chips,** or **chunks**). These come in three sizes—minichips, regular (best for most cookies), and maxichips. A caution: Read the label. Some ''baking chips'' are made with synthetic or imitation chocolate whose flavor isn't in the same league with the real thing.

**Cocoa** for baking can be either regular **unsweetened cocoa** powder (beware of cocoa mixes, which are mostly sugar) or **Dutch-process cocoa,** which I prefer. This has been given an alkali treatment that darkens its color while mellowing and deepening its flavor. Familiar brands, both imported, include Droste and Van Houten. The label indicates whether a cocoa has been "Dutched."

## NUTS: BUYING, STORING, AND PREPARING THEM FOR USE

To be sure that you're getting fresh nuts that can be kept in the cupboard for months without deteriorating (so long as they're unopened), the best bet is shelled nuts in vacuum-sealed cans. The selection isn't complete—I've never found hazelnuts packed this way, for instance—but the quality is excellent.

Be cautious about freshness when you buy shelled nuts from any source. Although it's convenient to purchase blanched, sliced, or chopped nuts in the little cellophane bags on supermarket racks, those bags have often been hanging around far too long. Nuts in the shell

are nearly always satisfactory when they're bought from a merchant whose stock has high turnover. (Don't overlook mail-order companies, too, for high-quality shelled pecans and almonds.)

Store both shelled and unshelled nuts in airtight containers in the freezer, where they will remain in good condition for months. If you lack freezer space, try to refrigerate the nuts, at least; it makes a remarkable difference in preserving their quality.

**Almonds** are often blanched after shelling to remove their barklike brown skin. (However, "natural" or unblanched almonds are often specified in recipes, and they can be substituted for blanched nuts in any recipe, if you prefer them.)

To blanch (or skin) almonds, pour enough boiling water over them to cover by an inch or so. Let the nuts stand for 2 minutes, then drain and pop them out of their skins between fingers and thumb.

Freshly blanched almonds tend to be rubbery. To dry them out, spread them on a baking sheet and leave them for a day or longer in an oven warmed only by a pilot light. Or, if you are in a hurry, turn the oven to its "warm" setting (or to no more than 175°F) and bake the almonds, stirring them often, until they have dried enough to be crisp, about 30 minutes.

To toast almonds for added nuttiness, follow the directions given with the recipe for Almond Cookies, More or Less

Chinese, page 94. If you're toasting unblanched natural almonds, keep a sharp eye on them, as it's impossible to see whether they are turning golden brown inside that golden-brown skin; to be sure, test one now and again.

**Hazelnuts** or **filberts** are still clad in a brown skin after they have been shelled. It's not essential to remove the skin, but, for the sake of appearance, many cooks prefer to do so. Directions for skinning hazelnuts accompany the recipe for Hazelnut-Raisin Mounds, page 54.

**Walnuts** and **pecans** don't require skinning. When nuts are an incidental, as in brownies, these two are interchangeable in recipes.

**Coconut,** which isn't a nut except in name, is most conveniently bought in airtight bags or vacuum-sealed cans. The recipes call for flaked coconut, which is decidedly moist and also considerably sweetened. Regular shredded coconut, or even home-grated fresh coconut, can be substituted. But bear in mind that the cookies will be less sweet if you crack and grate your own. To toast coconut, see the recipe for Kiss Kissies, page 74.

**Sesame seeds** are even less nutlike than coconut, but they're included here because they should be treated in the same way as nuts. Be cagey about buying them if you think they've been on the shelf a while—they are easy prey to rancidity. Taste before you buy, if possible. Buy hulled seeds (unhulled bagsful are often found at health food stores) to avoid a slight bitter edge in flavor. Store them in the freezer in an airtight jar; there's no need to thaw them before measuring.

# RAISINS AND OTHER FRUITS

Either **dark** or **light raisins** are fine for any cookie calling for raisins, but you'll find that the dark ones are more flavorful than the bleached variety. Golden raisins, however, are more attractive in certain cookies. **Dried currants,** if you have some around, can be substituted for raisins, measure for measure.

**Candied fruits** should be of very good quality; supermarket brands are seldom as good as they should be. It's easy to candy your own orange peel (page 77), and the same method can be used for grapefruit and lemon peel.

**Dried apricots, figs,** and **prunes** enter into some of the sweetmeats in this

book. Prunes of fine quality are in supermarkets, but apricots and figs are often specialty-store items. Try to taste, and don't be overly penny-wise; if dried fruits are not of high quality—apricots, especially—they aren't worth whatever they may cost.

**Dates** that have a bit of life and crunch (actually!) are preferable to the old-style "dried" dates that were squashed together into a block. They can be had pitted or whole.

# FLAVORINGS

Some of the flavorings, bottled and otherwise, that are used in the tiniest amounts have disproportionate impact. Therefore, quality counts, and so does care in measuring, especially when you are using the most concentrated flavors.

**Vanilla:** Please buy pure vanilla extract, not imitation vanilla, if you care about your cookies. Choose a reliable brand of all other flavorings, such as **almond, peppermint,** and **lemon;** and when you buy **maple** flavoring (which can be substituted for vanilla in any plain cookie), be sure you aren't getting the very powerful concentrate used for making inexpensive "maple" syrup at home. Measure carefully when using any liquid flavoring, but be especially careful with almond, lemon, and peppermint. They are decidedly outspoken, so much so that a few excess drops can play hob with the balance of flavors. Which proves that "Less is more" can be true in the kitchen, too.

**Coffee powder** or **crystals:** For the darkest, deepest coffee flavor, try dark-roast coffee powder.

**Spices** found on kitchen shelves often fade in flavor before anyone really notices. Have a sniff—has the ground spice you're about to use lost its youthful bloom? When in doubt, throw it out. If you must use it before it can be replaced, step up the quantity a bit.

**Orange** and **lemon rind:** Grate this fresh from bright-skinned fruit, taking care not to include the underlying white pith. The delicious aroma of the peel will tell you why the outer layer is called "zest." Dehydrated citrus peel should not be considered as a replacement.

**Liquors and wines:** When mixed into doughs to be baked, such potables as *dark rum, brandy, sherry,* and *Bourbon whiskey* are flavorings, rather than boozy nips, so teetotaling cooks needn't be concerned; the alcohol vanishes during baking. The real liquor or wine is preferable as a flavoring to the candidly labeled "imitation" liquor flavors.

**Peanut butter,** in my opinion, can never be too chunky—I sometimes add some chopped peanuts to what I scoop from the jar.

# TECHNIQUES

Recipes are easier to follow if you know the precise meaning of certain basic terms. Here are some used throughout the book; skip this if you are experienced.

## MIXING OPERATIONS— HAND METHODS

**To cream,** as in "cream the butter," means to mash and rub butter or other shortening vigorously against the sides of the bowl with the back of a big wooden (or metal) spoon, until it is uniformly soft and creamy. The fat should be at room temperature before attempting this.

**To cream in** sugar or other dry ingredients is to add the sugar gradually to creamed shortening while continuing with the creaming action; the aim is to make a light mixture. When eggs or other liquid ingredients are added to a creamed mixture, the operation changes to beating or stirring.

**To beat** is to use a spoon or a whisk in an over-and-over motion, so as to trace an imaginary circle through the food and the space above it. When beating, turn the bowl slightly after every few strokes to insure uniform mixing.

**To stir** is to move the spoon or whisk around and around the bowl in a gentler motion than beating; the circular pattern made by the spoon is in the same plane as the bowl rim. Turn the bowl occasionally as you stir.

**To whisk** is to beat with a whisk, or to stir briskly with a whisk, whichever makes sense for the food you're preparing. (Egg whites would be beaten; a batter would be stirred.) Turn the bowl occasionally as you whisk.

**To mix** means to stir or beat slowly or, in fact, to use the spoon, whisk, spatula, or other implement in whatever way combines the ingredients most successfully. "Mix" is often the direction when stiff doughs are involved. Some fine cooks use their well-scrubbed hands, one of the best tools of all.

**To fold** one mixture or ingredient into another, spoon or pour the second preparation over the first in the mixing bowl. With a rubber spatula, cut down through the two layers vertically. As the spatula reaches the bottom, turn its blade toward you and bring it to the surface, laying (or folding) a portion of the underlayer over the upper one. Repeat the folding motion, turning the bowl slightly after each fold, until the mixtures are sufficiently combined. To keep a batter as light as possible, be careful not to overdo folding—stop just as soon as no streaks of either mixture are to be seen in the batter.

**To cut in** means to combine butter or other solid fat with a flour mixture in such a way as to form fat and flour particles of the size desired. To the dry ingredients, add the chunks of fat (which should be very cold) and toss them for a moment to coat them with flour. Then, using a pastry blender, cut repeatedly through the bowl's contents, turning the bowl often, until the particles are the size described in the recipe. Alternatively, use two table knives, one in each hand, held with the blades close together and criss-crossing rapidly like scissors until the fat-flour particles are the right size. Stir the mixture with the knife tips and turn the bowl occasionally as you work.

# MIXING OPERATIONS— MACHINE METHODS

Creaming, beating, stirring, and cutting in can be performed by a properly equipped electric mixer and by all food processors, if you follow the manufacturer's instructions for your machine. However, I'd advise a beginning baker to make doughs and batters by hand and venture into machine use only after getting the hang of the process done the old way. Machines can't do everything; folding, for instance, can't be reproduced; most experienced cooks would always fold by hand, even if preliminary creaming and mixing had been done by machine.

# MEASURING HOW-TO'S

Using standard cups and spoons discussed under Equipment (page 9), it isn't hard to achieve measuring accuracy, which is more important in baking than in any other branch of cookery.

**Dry ingredients,** including flours of all kinds, sugar, and so on, should always be measured in dry-measuring cups. It's also more convenient to use these cups for brown sugar, solid shortening, dried fruit, and nuts, because you simply level the top for an accurate measurement. Before measuring flour, stir it well in its container, then dip in the cup, lift it with more than enough flour, and scrape off the excess with the edge of a straight knife or spatula. If the recipe specifies sifted flour, shake the flour through a sieve (or use a sifter) onto a sheet of waxed paper or a plate. Then spoon it *lightly* into the cup, without shaking it or allowing it to settle, and scrape off the excess with the edge of a knife or a metal spatula.

**Liquid or moist ingredients** should be measured in transparent liquid-measuring cups; hold the cup at eye level to check the amount.

**Small amounts** of ingredients are measured with full and fractional standard tablespoon and teaspoon measures. For measuring a "pinch," fingers replace a spoon: Pick up the ingredient with two fingers and a thumb, so that it amounts to about half of ⅛ teaspoon. Alternatively, if your measuring spoon set includes ⅛ teaspoon, fill and level it, then divide the contents in half with the tip of a knife. Push out one half and what remains is your pinch.

## Sifting, Pro and Con

On the question of whether or not to sift flour before measuring it, experts take more than two positions. Some rely on the words "presifted" on the label of the flour bag (I don't) and measure the flour without stirring it; others (myself included) stir the flour, especially if it has been sitting for a time in its container, then measure. If sifted flour is specified for an especially delicate mixture see the procedure described above among the measuring how-to's.

Sifting all the dry ingredients together is a step that shouldn't be skipped, if it is called for. If you have a flour sifter, measure the ingredients directly into it and sift them onto waxed paper or a plate. Lacking a sifter, measure the dry ingredients into a bowl and stir them together thoroughly with a whisk. Then shake the mixture through a sieve to remove any lumps.

## Chopping

Recipes indicate whether nuts, raisins, or other cut-up ingredients should be chopped to a fine, or medium, or coarse texture. In terms of a single raisin, "fine" would mean cutting it into 4 or 5 bits; "coarse" would mean 2 pieces; and medium (for other foods) would fall between. It's seldom a crucial point.

Almost any chopping operation can be carried out on a board using a heavy chef's knife with a 10-inch or 12-inch blade, or a Chinese cleaver if your fancy runs to those excellent knives. Other possibilities are using a manual or electric food grinder; a food processor (see its instruction manual); and, for a few things, a blender.

## Grating

This is most easily done, if you're dealing with orange or lemon rind, with a box grater, a stand-up affair with openings of various sizes on its four sides. When grating off the outer layer (zest) of citrus, be careful not to grate deeply into the white pith that lies under the bright skin; it can be bitter.

## Preparing Pans

The phrase "grease the pan" has been used deliberately to indicate that solid shortening, not butter, is the "grease" of choice. "Butter" may sound more attractive, but butter and margarine are not ideal for the purpose; they can burn (for instance, between cookies on a large pan), and experience shows that butter, especially if it contains too much moisture, can cause bar cookies to stick. When the direction is to "grease and flour" the pan, spread a thin coating of shortening over the baking surface (wipe it on with a piece of paper toweling), then sprinkle about a tablespoonful of flour into the pan or onto the baking sheet. Next, tilt the pan briskly in all directions until the greased surface has been coated. Invert the pan and knock on its bottom to remove excess flour.

# SHAPING COOKIES

**Drop cookies** are formed by dropping dough from the tip of a spoon (or even a cup, in the case of Monsters). Using a fingertip or another spoon, push the indicated amount of dough onto the bak-

ing sheet. A small rubber spatula is good for pushing, too.

**Molded cookies,** in this book, are most often made by rolling a portion of dough between your palms into a ball. If the dough begins to stick to your hands, scrape off any that has adhered and wipe your palms dry. This shouldn't happen if the dough is of the right consistency. If it should be too moist, a little flour can be worked in to correct the problem. When balls of dough are to be flattened, the recipe tells how.

**Icebox cookies:** Well, I suppose they're refrigerator cookies, but that name is much less inviting—are formed by cutting thin slices from a chilled cylinder of dough. The only helpful hint here is to try to cut the slices of uniform thickness for each panful so the cookies will all be done at once; you can please yourself about making the cookies thinner or thicker than the recipe suggests, but I'd try a few "as written" first.

**Rolled and cut cookies:** As a category, this includes some tricky customers. To simplify the process of making them successfully, I have suggested that dough be rolled between two sheets of plastic wrap. Center the dough on one sheet of wrap, cover it with a second, and pat it out to an oval an inch or so thick. Then roll with a rolling pin, changing directions now and again for uniform thickness.

Turn back the plastic and check the thickness of the rolled-out dough with a cake tester, thin skewer, or cocktail pick. To do so, pierce the dough with the pointed device, held upright, and place the tip of your thumbnail exactly at the surface of the dough. Withdraw the object with thumb in place and measure the distance from the tip to your thumbnail with the ruler.

Peel off the upper sheet of plastic completely and cut the cookies as the recipe directs. For easy transfer of the cut shapes, pull away the dough between them and set it aside for re-rolling, then carefully transfer each cookie to the baking sheet or otherwise continue with the recipe.

To cut wafer shapes, use a pastry wheel or a jagger or employ a ruler (or a straight-edge) and a sharp knife.

**Bar cookies** aren't shaped at all but rather baked in a slab, then cut apart.

**Using a pastry bag.** This device is far from necessary to any kitchen, but it does form the prettiest of drop cookies, especially macaroons. Here's how.

Use a medium-size pastry bag, about 12 inches in length, and fit it with a large plain tube or a large star tube. Fold back about half of the bag and prop it, tube downward, in a tall jar or other narrow container, with the turned-back "cuff" outside the jar. Transfer the cookie dough to the pastry bag with a rubber spatula, filling the bag about

halfway. Twist the top closed and hold the bag in one hand by the twisted portion. Guide the tip with the other hand while continuing to twist the "neck" to press out cookies of the size you want onto the baking sheet. If you should make a mistake and shape a too-huge cookie, it's a simple matter to scrape up the dough and try again.

## TIMING THE BAKING

This discussion could be entitled "My time is your time . . . maybe." Which is to say that baking times indicated in recipes can never be more than an educated approximation. The reason? No two ovens perform exactly alike and, further, oven controls are notoriously unreliable. Hence the suggestions in Equipment, page 11, that you use both an oven thermometer and a timer.

**Judging doneness:** When making any cookies—and especially if you're using a recipe for the first time—watch them for signs of doneness, beginning several minutes before the minimum baking time is up. When their appearance, or other tests suggested in the recipe, indicate that they're done, remove them promptly from the oven.

Some ways to recognize doneness: *By color*—the degree of browning of tops and rims, for example. *By touch*—how firm a cookie should feel is indicated, when this test is appropriate. *By behavior during baking*—some cookies that will end up with a crackled surface will puff up while baking, then collapse and become sufficiently firm, all in a minute or two. *By use of a cake tester*—these little gadgets are used to pierce the center of a panful of brownies and some other bar cookies. If the tester emerges clean and dry, the batch is done.

**Brownie time(s):** Overbaked brownies are often hard and dry, but slightly underbaked brownies are deliciously chewy, a state preferred by some. If you like them chewy, cut 5 minutes from the suggested baking time or, alternatively, take the pan from the oven while the center of the brownies still yields to a light touch and the sides have scarcely begun to draw away from the pan.

**Cooling the cookies:** Whether they come off the pan at once, or stay in place for a few minutes to firm up (or even to cool completely) depends on the type and size of the cookies. Most brownies should be cooled completely in the pan before they are cut, to prevent dryness. However, certain other bars should be cut while slightly warm (the recipe will so indicate). Use a metal spatula to transfer small cookies to cooling racks. All cookies should be completely cooled before they are stored.

## CUT-UPS

Before cutting the finished bar cookies, run a knife around the edges to free the block from the sides of the pan. Use a serrated knife for neat cutting, and a small metal spatula for lifting bars from the pan. Choose a serrated knife for tidy slicing of Fruit Newts (page 120), too.

## WRAP SESSION: PROTECTING MONSTERS AND OTHERS

Oversize cookies, monster size or larger, should be wrapped individually to protect them against accidents, especially if they're intended for gift-giving or for sale at a fund-raiser.

The 6-inch Monster cookies can safely be wrapped in plastic alone and boxed or stacked (with care). It can do no harm to back each one with a round of heavy-duty foil before wrapping, however.

Maximonsters and Ultimates should be given a backing of thin cardboard or two thicknesses of heavy-duty foil. If foil is used, cut it a little larger than the cookie and bend it up around the sides for a fraction of an inch. Wrap the whole works in plastic, holding it in place on the back with a strip or two of tape.

**Shrink wrapping:** This is an attractive way to let your cookies shine; it keeps them fresh while showing off their good looks. You'll need good-quality plastic wrap (thin ''bargain'' wrap won't work—it melts instead of shrinking); cookies that have been backed with cardboard or foil as described above; a baking sheet; and some paper towels.

Turn on the oven and set it at 325°F. Cover a large baking sheet with two layers of paper towels and set it aside. Carefully wrap each cardboard- or foil-backed cookie in plastic (if necessary, use overlapping sheets to cover the largest size); fold the excess plastic flat against the back of the cookie. Then set the baking sheet, with the toweling, in the oven and leave it until it is quite warm, almost hot. At that point, set a cookie or two on the toweling and stand right there, oven door open, watching, while the plastic shrinks to snugness (all this takes only seconds). Remove the cookie and check on the back; if necessary, return the cookie to the pan for an instant to ''seal'' the plastic folds (or simply run a piece of tape across the ends). That's it. Overwrap shrink-

wrapped cookies with foil if they are to be frozen; thaw them in the foil wrapping.

## Storing Cookies

For room-temperature storage, cookie jars, canisters, or plastic kitchen containers (with lids) are all useful. Plastic bags or wrap and aluminum foil can also be used. To keep crisp cookies crisp (barring extra-humid weather, in which case *all* cookies tend to become soft), be sure not to close the cookie container tightly; a slight air exchange preserves their texture. On the other hand, soft cookies and chewy types should be closed airtight. (Never mix types in a container unless you want both kinds to suffer in texture and flavor.) Bar cookies are most conveniently stored in their baking pan, which should be covered tightly with plastic wrap or foil.

If in spite of careful storage crisp cookies should soften, revive them by placing them, on a rack or baking sheet, in a 300°F oven for a few minutes. (This treatment also freshens other types of cookies.) Cool them before serving.

Soft or chewy cookies that are hardening in spite of correct storage can be rescued by enclosing half an apple or a slice of fresh bread with them. Remove the ''humidifier'' in a day or two, replacing it with another, if necessary.

**Refrigerator storage:** If the recipe okays refrigerator storage, use a tightly covered container, tightly closed plastic bags, or a close wrapping of plastic wrap or foil.

## The Big Sleep—Freezing

Almost all cookies freeze satisfactorily; however, follow the recipe recommendations, as there are one or two kinds (such as macaroons) that don't take kindly to the deep-freeze. Package cookies in freezer-weight plastic bags, expelling as much air as possible; or use rigid plastic freezer containers (with covers), or a close wrapping of foil or plastic wrap plus a seal of tape on the seams.

Some frozen cookies—brownies come to mind—are perfectly delicious to eat while still frozen or at most semi-thawed. Most others should be thawed, however. To preserve their texture, try to thaw them in their wrappers; unwrapped, frozen cookies can attract moisture from the air and become soggy. Refreshing cookies in the oven, as described above, is a good plan when they have been frozen. They needn't be thawed first.

# THE MONSTERS

Including Minimonsters, Maximonsters, and even Ultimate Monsters.

# CLASSIC CHOCOLATE CHIP COOKIES

**B**ig enough to serve as a birthday cookie (with a candle in the middle), one of these can also feed a whole posse of hungry friends, or it can be doled out to yourself in daily chunks for a cookie fix that can last a week. Each of the finished cookies of the largest size weighs about a pound—it is the heaviest of the maxis— and is 9 inches, or a bit over, in diameter. This chocolate-chipper for Gargantua, when shrunken down to cookie shop size (the smallest), is very similar to the classic prototype baked years ago at a Massachusetts inn called the Toll House. Logically enough, when innkeeper Ruth Wakefield's cookies caught on so widely that chocolate bits of the right size were marketed especially for making them, they became known as ''Toll House Cookies.'' Today there are countless chocolate chip variations, some of them to be found in these pages, but no other type has toppled the original from first place; it's still the champ. A proper chocolate chip cookie can be made with or without nuts. If you want their crunch, add a cupful of coarsely chopped walnuts, stirring them in with the chocolate pieces.

½ cup (1 stick) unsalted butter, at room temperature

¼ cup vegetable shortening, at room temperature

½ cup (packed) light brown sugar

½ cup granulated sugar

2 eggs

2 teaspoons vanilla extract

1½ cups all-purpose flour

½ teaspoon baking soda

½ teaspoon baking powder

½ teaspoon salt

2 cups (a 12-ounce package) semisweet chocolate pieces

**1.** Prepare foil bases for the maxi size (this dough is somewhat soft and the cookies are more shapely if baked in a rounded ''pan'' or mold made of aluminum foil). To make the molds, cut two 12-inch squares of heavy-duty aluminum foil. Press each sheet around the base of a pot or skillet about 11 inches in diameter. Trim the upstanding edge to ½ inch, leaving a shallow pan. Set each on a baking sheet and lightly grease the bottom. Using a plate or pan as a pattern, mark an 8-inch circle on the greased surface with your fingertip. If you're baking small cookies, cover one or two baking sheets with foil and grease the foil lightly.

**2.** In a mixing bowl (using a wooden spoon) or in the large bowl of an electric mixer, cream the butter and shortening together until well blended and soft. Then beat in the brown and granulated sugars in turn, beating well after each addition, until fluffy. Add the eggs one at a time, beating well after each; then beat in the vanilla.

**3.** Sift together the flour, baking soda, baking powder, and salt. Stir the flour mixture into the creamed mixture, blending well. Add the chocolate bits, reserving ½ cup if you're baking maxi-cookies, and mix well. Wrap the dough in plastic wrap and chill it thoroughly, preferably for 3 hours or longer. (It keeps well for at least three days.)

**4.** Preheat the oven to 350°F, with oven rack in the center position.

## Form and Bake the Cookies

**5.** *To make 9-inch maximonsters:* Divide the dough in half for these huge cookies. Heap each half in the center of the ring marked on the foil. With your fingers or a rubber spatula, pat the dough out into a neat circle inside the marking. Scatter half of the reserved chocolate pieces over each cookie and poke the bits partly into the dough. Bake the cookies one at a time in the preheated oven for 25 to 30 minutes, until they are lightly browned and the center has become springy when touched lightly. Slide the molds and their cookies onto wire racks and cool them completely. If the edges have spread slightly and are overbrowned, trim them neatly while the cookies are still warm.

**6.** *To make 6-inch monsters:* Measure the chilled dough in a ⅓-cup measure, leveling the top. Space the dough about 3 inches apart on the foil-covered greased baking sheet (step 1). Flatten the mounds with the palm and fingers of your hand or a rubber spatula to a 3- to 3½-inch diameter. Bake the cookies in the preheated oven for 12 to 15 minutes, or until they are lightly browned and the centers are springy when touched lightly. Slide the foil off the sheet and cool the cookies on the foil for 5 minutes, then place them on wire racks to cool completely.

**7.** *To make 2-inch cookies:* Drop the chilled dough by slightly rounded measuring teaspoonfuls onto the foil-covered greased sheet (step 1), spacing them 2 inches apart. Bake them in the preheated oven for 8 to 10 minutes, until they are lightly browned and the centers have just become springy to the touch. Slide the foil off the sheet and cool the cookies on the foil for 5 minutes, then place them on wire racks to cool completely.

**8.** When the cookies have cooled, wrap or bag them, or place them in a covered container, and store them at room temperature for a few days, or in the refrigerator for longer keeping. The maximonsters should be backed by a round of thin cardboard or two layers of heavy-duty aluminum foil as insurance against breakage. Any of the cookies may be frozen. If they have been frozen they benefit from a 5- to 10-minute warming in a 300°F oven (they need not be thawed first). Cool them again before they are served.

*Makes 2 maximonster cookies about 9 inches in diameter; or about 12 6-inch monster cookies; or about 5 dozen 2-inch cookies*

# DOUBLE-CHOCOLATE RAISIN AND CHIP COOKIES

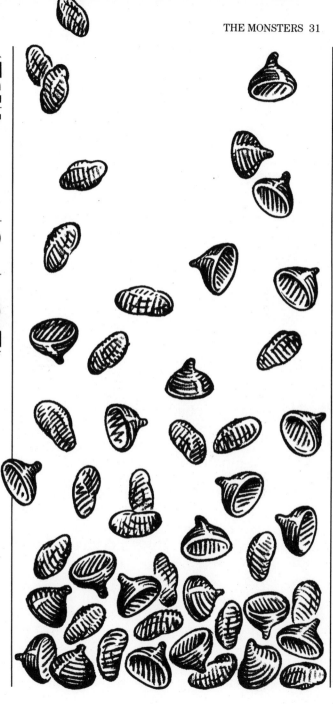

Raisins as well as chocolate bits embedded in a rich chocolaty dough distinguish these particular members of the chip-cookie tribe. The recipe can be varied—you might want to omit the cocoa from the dough (increase the flour by 2 tablespoons if you do that), and nuts can be substituted for (or added to) the raisins in either the dark or pale cookies.

½ cup (1 stick) unsalted butter, at room
    temperature
¼ cup vegetable shortening
¾ cup (packed) dark brown sugar
¾ cup granulated sugar
2 eggs
1 teaspoon vanilla extract
2 cups all-purpose flour
½ cup unsweetened cocoa, preferably
    Dutch-process
1 teaspoon salt
1 teaspoon baking soda
2 cups (a 12-ounce package) semisweet
    chocolate pieces
1 to 1½ cups raisins

**1.** In a mixing bowl (using a wooden spoon) or in the large bowl of an electric mixer, cream the butter and shortening together until soft and completely mixed. Add, in turn, the brown sugar and the granulated sugar, beating after each addition until fluffy. Beat in the eggs one at a time, and add the vanilla.

**2.** Sift together the flour, cocoa, salt, and baking soda. Stir the flour mixture into the creamed mixture, then add the chocolate pieces and raisins and stir them in. Wrap the dough and chill it thoroughly, preferably for 3 hours or longer. (It will keep for several days under refrigeration.)

**3.** Preheat the oven to 350°F, with an oven rack in the center position. Cover a baking sheet with aluminum foil and grease the foil. (You'll need extra sheets of lightly greased foil for subsequent batches.)

## Form and Bake the Cookies

**4.** *To make 9-inch maximonsters:* Divide the dough into three equal portions. Using a pot lid or baking pan as a pattern, mark an 8-inch circle into the greased surface of the foil-covered baking sheet. Place a portion of dough in the center of the marked area and spread it evenly with the fingers and heel of your hand or a rubber spatula. (If you have only one baking sheet, while the first cookie bakes form the second and third cookies on individual sheets of greased foil, then slip each sheet in turn onto the baking sheet after it has cooled down.) If you want to bake fewer than three maximonsters, measure out 1 cup of dough for each one, and form smaller cookies out of the rest (steps 5 and 6). Bake the maximonsters, one at a time, in the center of the preheated oven for about 20 minutes. The cookies are done when they have puffed and then subsided to make a crackled surface and are just semifirm when touched in the center. Slide the sheet of foil onto a wire rack and cool the cookie completely.

**5.** *To make 6-inch monsters:* Use a ⅓-cup measure to shape portions of dough, leveling the top. Place three portions, as far apart as possible, on each baking sheet covered with greased foil. Flatten them out to a 5-inch diameter, using the fingers and heel of your hand or a rubber spatula dipped in sugar. Bake for 13 to 15 minutes, or until done as described for maximonsters in step 4. Slide the foil off the baking sheet, cool the cookies for 5 minutes on the foil, then remove them to a wire rack to cool completely. The foil may be reused for another batch. (Be sure to let the baking sheets and foil cool completely before using them again.)

**6.** *To make 3½-inch cookies:* Make 1-inch balls of the chilled dough and place them about 3 inches apart on a sheet covered with greased foil. Flatten each to about 2 inches in diameter, using the heel of the hand or a rubber spatula dipped in sugar. Bake the cookies for 12 to 14

minutes, or until done as described in step 4. Slide the foil off the baking sheet and cool the cookies on the foil for 5 minutes, then remove them to wire racks to cool completely.

**7.** When the cookies are completely cool, wrap them or place them in a covered container or plastic bag and store them at room temperature for a few days, or in the refrigerator for longer keeping. The maximonsters should be backed by a round of thin cardboard, or two layers of heavy-duty foil, as reinforcement before wrapping them for gift-giving or storage. These cookies also freeze well, either bagged or wrapped.

***Makes*** *3 maximonster cookies about 9 inches in diameter; or about 20 6-inch monster cookies; or about 4 dozen 3½-inch cookies*

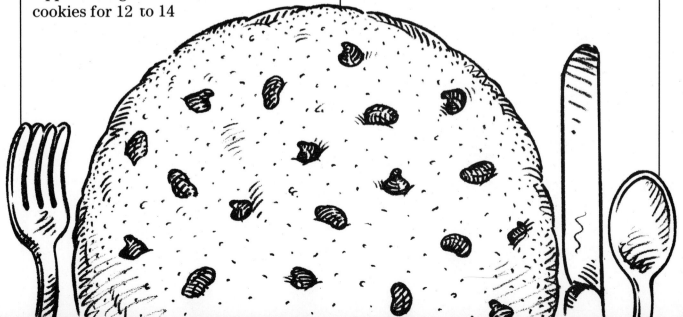

# MOCHA WALNUT CHOCOLATE CHIP COOKIES

Coffee enriches the chocolate batter of these deliciously dark cookies, which are studded with walnuts and choco-

late chips. A gift-wrapped maxicookie, pushing a pound in weight and upwards of 9 inches in diameter, would be the ultimate gift for any mochaphile.

*¼ cup (½ stick) unsalted butter, at room temperature*

*¼ cup vegetable shortening, at room temperature*

*½ cup (packed) dark brown sugar*

*½ cup granulated sugar*

*1 egg*

*½ teaspoon vanilla extract*

*1 cup all-purpose flour*

*¼ cup unsweetened cocoa, preferably Dutch-process*

*2 tablespoons instant coffee powder (if in crystal form, crush to powder before measuring)*

*½ teaspoon salt*

*½ teaspoon baking soda*

*1½ cups (9 ounces) semisweet chocolate pieces*

*½ to 1 cup coarsely chopped walnuts*

**1.** Preheat the oven to 350°F, with an oven rack in the center position. Cover one or more baking sheets with aluminum foil and grease the foil.

**2.** In a mixing bowl (using a wooden spoon) or in the large bowl of an electric mixer, cream the butter and shortening together until soft and completely mixed. Add the brown sugar and granulated sugar in turn, beating well after each addition. Add the egg and the vanilla and beat again.

**3.** Sift together the flour, cocoa, coffee powder, salt, and baking soda. Stir the flour mixture into the creamed mixture until well blended. Stir in the chocolate pieces and the walnuts.

## Form and Bake the Cookies

**4.** *To make 9-inch maximonsters:* Divide the dough in half. Using a pot lid or round baking pan as a pattern, mark with a fingertip an 8-inch circle into the greased surface of a foil–covered baking sheet. Place half of the dough in the center of the circle and spread it evenly over the marked area with your hand or a rubber spatula. Bake one cookie at a time in the center of the preheated oven for 18 to 20 minutes. The cookie is done after it has puffed, then subsided to become crackled; the center will yield slightly when touched lightly. Slide the sheet of foil onto a wire rack and cool the cookie on the foil as a precaution against breakage.

**5.** *To make 6-inch monsters:* Measure the dough for each in a ⅓-cup measure, leveling the top. Place three portions on each foil-covered baking sheet, spacing the cookies well apart. Flatten the dough to a 5-inch diameter with your

hand or a rubber spatula dipped in sugar. Bake the cookies 16 to 18 minutes, or until the indications given in step 4 show that they are done. Slide the foil off the sheets, cool the cookies for 5 minutes, then place them, still on the foil, on wire racks to cool completely.

**6.** *To make 2½- to 3-inch cookies:* Using a measuring teaspoon, drop rounded spoonfuls of dough about 3 inches apart on the foil-covered baking sheet. Flatten the mounds slightly with the heel of your hand, or use a rubber spatula dipped in sugar. Bake the cookies in the preheated oven for about 12 minutes, until they are done according to the indications in step 4. Slide the foil off the sheets, cool the cookies on the foil for 5 minutes, then remove them to wire racks to cool completely.

**7.** When the cookies have cooled, wrap or bag them in plastic or wrap them in aluminum foil, or place them in a covered container. Store the cookies at room temperature for a few days, or in the refrigerator for longer keeping. The biggest ones should be backed by a round of thin cardboard or two layers of heavy-duty aluminum foil as insurance against breakage. The cookies, suitably wrapped, may be frozen.

***Makes*** *2 maximonster cookies, about 9 inches in diameter; or 10 to 12 6-inch monster cookies; or about 3 dozen 2½- to 3-inch cookies*

# PEANUT BUTTER CHOCOLATE CHIP COOKIES

**W**hether it's the child or the adult in each of us who recognizes the affinity of peanut butter and chocolate, all ages agree that they are meant for each other. For these drop cookies, choose the chunkiest brand of peanut butter you can find, if you like to experience real crunch alongside meltingly soft chocolate.

½ cup (1 stick) unsalted butter, at room temperature
¾ cup chunk-style peanut butter
½ cup (packed) light brown sugar
½ cup granulated sugar
2 eggs
3 tablespoons orange juice or water
1 teaspoon vanilla extract
1½ cups all-purpose flour
1 teaspoon baking soda
½ teaspoon baking powder
¼ teaspoon salt
1 to 1½ cups (6 to 9 ounces) semisweet chocolate pieces

**1.** Preheat the oven to 350°F, with an oven rack in the center position. Lightly grease one or two baking sheets if making small cookies. For the larger sizes, cover a baking sheet with aluminum foil and grease it lightly. (You'll need extra sheets of lightly greased foil for subsequent batches.)

**2.** In a mixing bowl (using a wooden spoon) or in the large bowl of an electric mixer, cream the butter with the peanut butter until the mixture is soft. Beat in the brown sugar, then the granulated sugar, beating after each addition until the mixture is light. Beat in the eggs one at a time, then beat in the orange juice or water and vanilla.

**3.** Sift together the flour, baking soda, baking powder, and salt. Fold the flour mixture into the creamed mixture, then stir in the chocolate pieces.

## Form and Bake the Cookies

**4.** *To make 9-inch maximonsters:* Divide the dough into four equal portions. Using a 7-inch pot lid or round baking pan as a pattern, mark with a fingertip a circle onto the greased surface of each foil-covered baking sheet. (If you have only one baking sheet, form the dough for subsequent cookies on sheets of greased foil, then slip each in turn onto the cooled sheet after each baking.) Heap each portion in the center of the ring marked on the foil. With your hand or a rubber spatula, pat the dough for each cookie out into a neat circle inside the marking. Bake the cookies one at a time. If you want to bake fewer than four maximonsters, measure out 1 cup of dough for each one (shaping them as above) and form smaller cookies out of the rest (steps 5 and 6). Bake each maximonster in the preheated oven for about 15 to 16 minutes, or until it is golden brown and the center is just firm. Cool on the baking sheet for at least 5 minutes, then slide the foil, with the cookie, onto a wire rack to cool completely.

**5.** *To make 6-inch monsters:* Measure the dough for each cookie in a ⅓-cup measure, with the top leveled. Place three portions of dough on each foil-covered baking sheet, spacing the cookies well apart. Flatten each mound to just under a 4-inch diameter with your hand or a rubber spatula. Bake for about 14 minutes or until done as described for maximonsters in step 4. Cool the cookies on the baking sheet for at least 5 minutes, then slide the foil, with the cookies, onto a wire rack to cool completely.

**6.** *To make 2½-inch cookies:* Drop the dough by rounded teaspoonfuls onto the greased baking sheet, spacing them about 2 inches apart, and flatten the mounds slightly with your hand or a rubber spatula. Bake the cookies for about 14 minutes, or until done as described for maximonsters in step 4. Cool the cookies on the sheet briefly, then lift them with a spatula onto a wire rack to cool completely.

**7.** When the cookies have cooled, wrap or bag them, or place them in a tightly covered container, and store at room temperature for a few days. Refrigerate or freeze them for longer storage. The maximonsters should be backed by a round of thin cardboard or two layers of heavy-duty aluminum foil as insurance against breakage. If the cookies have been frozen, they benefit from a 10-minute warming in a 300°F oven (they need not be thawed first). Cool them again before they are served.

*Makes 4 maximonster cookies about 9 inches in diameter; or 12 to 14 6-inch monster cookies; or about 5 dozen 2½-inch cookies*

# FOUR ULTIMATE COOKIES

The Ultimate Chocolate Chip Cookie—the most monstrous monster of all—12 inches in diameter and weighing around 1¾ pounds, depending on which dough is used.

What's the ultimate disposition of an Ultimate? They belong at picnics; they make stupendous gifts; they are dandy for raffling off at fundraisers; and, above all, they pack enough power to satisfy a whole family of cookie mavens for quite a spell. The directions that follow have been worked out for the four previous chocolate chip doughs.

COOKIE DOUGH

*1 recipe of any of the following:*

*Classic Chocolate Chip Cookies, page 28*

*Double-Chocolate Raisin and Chip Cookies, page 31*

*Mocha-Walnut Chocolate Chip Cookies, page 34*

*Peanut Butter-Chocolate Chip Cookies, page 36*

TOPPING

*½ to 1 cup (3 to 6 ounces) semisweet chocolate pieces*

**1.** *Prepare the dough* (and chill it if so directed) according to the recipe chosen.

**2.** When the dough is ready to bake, preheat the oven to 325°F, with an oven rack in the center position.

**3.** *Prepare the pan:* Line a 12-inch pizza pan with two sheets of regular-weight aluminum foil, crossing the sheets at right angles to cover the baking surface completely. Crimp the foil securely over the rim and cut away the excess. Grease the foil lightly, then trace a 10-inch circle in the coating, keeping it a uniform 1 inch away from the rim. (Use a pot lid or round baking pan as a pattern.) If you lack a pizza pan, form a 12-inch "pan" of two layers of heavy-duty foil, following the pan-making procedure outlined in the recipe for Classic Chocolate Chip Cookies. Set either the pizza pan or the foil stand-in on a large baking sheet. Grease the foil pan when it is in place, then trace a 10-inch circle in the fat.

**4.** *Form the cookie:* Measure 3 level cups of the dough into the center of the pattern on the baking pan. (Reserve the remainder and bake as smaller cookies—all the doughs will keep for several days in the refrigerator.) Using a rubber spatula or your fingers, spread the dough evenly over the marked area on the pan, making tidy edges. Do not smooth the top—it is more attractive if left somewhat rough. Sprinkle the extra chocolate pieces over the top of the cookie and press them in about halfway.

**5.** Bake the cookie in the center of the preheated oven according to the following time schedule, checking on doneness several minutes before the cookie is expected to be done. (The foil covering called for below is a single sheet of heavy-duty foil large enough to cover the cookie completely.)

**Classic Cookie:** Bake 25 minutes, then cover loosely with foil and bake an additional 15 to 20 minutes, until the cookie has puffed and fallen back and feels barely firm when touched lightly in the center. (The shorter time yields a chewier cookie; this is also true of the other three cookies here.)

**Double-Chocolate Raisin Cookie:** Bake the cookie for 20 minutes, then cover it loosely with foil and bake it for an additional 15 to 20 minutes, until it is barely firm when touched lightly in the center.

**Mocha-Walnut Cookie:** Bake 20 minutes, then cover the cookie loosely with foil and bake it an additional 15 to 20 minutes, or until it is barely firm when touched lightly in the center.

**Peanut Butter-Chocolate Cookie:** Bake the cookie for 20 minutes, then cover it loosely with foil and bake it an additional 20 to 25 minutes, until it is just firm when touched lightly in the center.

**6.** When the cookie is done, remove it, in its pan, from the baking sheet and cool it completely on a wire rack. When it is cool, trim the edges of the foil pan, leaving a slight turn-up all around. Back the cookie with a round of cardboard or another round of heavy-duty foil cut to fit, and wrap it in foil for storage. For an attractive appearance when the cookie is to be a gift or an offering at a bazaar, shrink-wrap it in plastic as described in "Wrap Session," page 24.

***Makes** a 12-inch cookie, with dough left over for making smaller cookies*

# CRACKLY ORANGE AND GINGER COOKIES

An old-fashioned bite, substantial to the tooth, fragrant and soul-warming. This recipe is a direct descendant of one used for a long lifetime by my Great-Aunt Minnie, whether she found herself living in exotic California or back home in Warren County, New Jersey. The orange rind in the cookies and in the coating sugar is my own Californian touch, as is the nut-coated variation suggested at the foot of the recipe.

*¾ cup vegetable shortening*

*1 cup (packed) light or dark brown sugar*

*½ cup unsulphured light molasses*

*1 egg*

*2 tablespoons finely grated orange rind (colored outer layer only, no pith)*

*2¼ cups all-purpose flour*

*1 tablespoon ground ginger*

*1 teaspoon ground cinnamon*

*2 teaspoons baking soda*

*½ teaspoon salt*

ORANGE SUGAR FOR COATING

*1 tablespoon finely grated orange rind (colored outer layer only, no pith)*

*½ cup granulated sugar*

**1.** Preheat the oven to 350°F, with an oven rack in the center position.

**2.** In a mixing bowl (using a wooden spoon) or in the large bowl of an electric mixer, cream the shortening until it is soft. Then add the sugar, beating until the mixture is fluffy. Beat in the molasses, then the egg, beating well after each addition, and finally add the 2 tablespoons of orange rind.

**3.** Sift together the flour, ginger, cinnamon, baking soda, and salt. Stir this mixture thoroughly into the creamed mixture.

**4.** *Make the orange sugar for coating:* In a bowl, combine thoroughly the 1 tablespoon of orange rind and the granulated sugar.

## Form and Bake the Cookies

**5.** *For 6-inch monsters:* Measure the dough for each cookie in a ⅓-cup measure, leveling the top. Shape the dough into a ball and roll it in the orange sugar, coating it well. Place the cookies on an ungreased baking sheet at least 3 inches apart, to allow space for spreading during baking. There should be 3 cookies per sheet.

**6.** *For 3-inch cookies:* For each cookie, scoop up a heaping measuring tablespoonful of the dough. Form it into a ball and drop it into a bowl containing the orange sugar, then turn it to coat it well. Place the coated ball on an ungreased baking sheet. Shape the remaining dough in the same manner, spacing the cookies 3 inches apart.

**7.** Bake the cookies in the center of the preheated oven for 12 minutes (for small cookies) to 15 minutes (for the larger size), or until the edges are firm and the centers have puffed and subsided (this forms the crackles). Cool the cookies on the baking sheet until they are firm, at least 5 minutes, then move them to wire racks to cool completely. These cookies, stored in a covered but not airtight container, keep perfectly for weeks at room temperature. They may also be frozen for longer storage.

***Makes*** *about 10 6-inch monster cookies, or about 4 dozen 3-inch cookies*

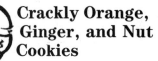

### Crackly Orange, Ginger, and Nut Cookies

Substitute ¼ cup of finely chopped walnuts or pecans for the orange rind (or use both) in the coating of sugar.

# FRUIT AND NUT PARTY PIZZAS

Overgrown sugar cookies playfully embellished with jam, nuts, coconut, dried fruits, or other goodies make a grand dessert for groups of the young in years (or heart). The "pizzas" are around 9 inches in diameter; if you prefer them smaller, make the smaller cookies described in the recipe for Big Sugars on page 56. If you want to make only one big "pizza," bake and shape the rest of the dough as either 3-inch or 7-inch cookies. (The dough, well wrapped, will keep for days in the refrigerator.)

*Chilled dough for Big Sugars, page 56*

GLAZE
*1 egg white*
*1½ teaspoons water*

TOPPINGS
*Your choice, any or all, for 3 "pizzas":*
*About 1 cup assorted dried fruit (apricots, peaches, prunes, pears, raisins)*
*About 1½ cups chunky berry jam, preferably strawberry (avoid runny jam)*
*About ½ cup flaked or grated coconut*
*About 1 cup sliced almonds, or sliced Brazil nuts, or coarsely chopped walnuts*

**1.** Preheat the oven to 400°F, with an oven rack in the center position.

**2.** For each "pizza" maximonster, lay out a 12-inch square of aluminum foil and grease it lightly. Place one foil square on a baking sheet.

**3.** Divide the chilled dough into three equal portions. Return two portions to the refrigerator while you shape the first one. Form the dough into a ball, place it on the foil-covered baking sheet, and flatten it with your hands to a diameter of 5 or 6 inches. Then, using the bottom of a glass pie plate or a heavy baking pan, flatten the dough further until it measures 8½ inches across. (If the pie plate sticks, sprinkle the underside with granulated sugar.) If the edge of the dough has cracked, tidy it by patting inward around the edge with the flat of a knife blade.

**4.** *Glaze the cookie:* Mix the egg white and water thoroughly and brush the top of the cookie with the mixture.

**5.** Bake the big cookie in the center of the preheated oven for about 10 minutes, until the top has puffed (it will fall again, either in or out of the oven) and the edges are golden brown. Set the baking sheet on a wire rack to cool for 5 minutes, then slip the foil, with the cookie, carefully onto the rack and cool the cookie completely.

**6.** Shape and bake the second and third portions of dough in turn, making sure that the baking sheet has cooled between trips to the oven.

**7.** If the cookies aren't to be garnished and served within a few hours, back them with cardboard or doubled aluminum foil, wrap them in aluminum foil or plastic wrap and store them at room temperature for a day or two. They may also be frozen.

**8.** *Topping the "pizzas":* Shortly before serving time, soak the dried fruits in warm water for about 15 minutes. Drain them, pat them dry, and cut them with scissors into strips or, in the case of raisins, into halves. Spread a layer of jam over each cookie, leaving a clear margin around the edge; about ½ cup of jam per "pizza" should be enough. Over the jam make whatever design you fancy, using the dried fruits, coconut, and nuts, or simply scatter the trimmings over the top in random strewings.

**9.** To serve, cut the fruit and nut "pizzas" into wedges, using a pastry wheel or pizza cutter. Leftovers are quite acceptable, if there are any, for a day or two; however, the crust will become a little mellower upon standing. Refrigerating or freezing the completed "pizzas" is not recommended.

*Makes 3 maxi-monster cookies about 9 inches in diameter*

# SPICED
## ORANGE-OATMEAL
# COOKIES

**B**lend a harmony of citrus and spice with a crunch of oats, and you have an intriguing cookie to bake in large or small rounds. Unlike some oat cookies, this one doesn't shatter easily after baking, so you can go for the maximonster size.

¾ cup vegetable shortening

¾ cup (packed) light brown sugar

¾ cup granulated sugar

2 eggs

2 tablespoons frozen concentrated orange juice, thawed but undiluted

3 tablespoons finely grated or chopped orange rind (colored outer layer only, no pith)

1½ cups all-purpose flour

1 teaspoon baking soda

1 teaspoon baking powder

1 teaspoon salt

1 teaspoon ground cinnamon

½ teaspoon ground allspice

½ teaspoon ground nutmeg

2½ cups regular (not quick-cooking) rolled oats

**1.** Preheat the oven to 350°F, with an oven rack in the center position. For the larger cookies, cover a baking sheet with aluminum foil and grease the foil lightly; you'll need another sheet of greased foil for each batch following the first. If you are making 3½-inch cookies, lightly grease one or two baking sheets.

**2.** In a mixing bowl (using a wooden spoon) or in the large bowl of an electric mixer, cream the shortening until soft. Beat in the brown sugar, then the granulated sugar, and beat until fluffy. Add the eggs one at a time, beating well after each addition. Beat in the orange juice concentrate and the orange rind.

**3.** Sift together the flour, baking soda, baking powder, salt, cinnamon, allspice, and nutmeg. Stir the flour mixture into the creamed mixture, combining them thoroughly. Add the oats, mixing well.

### Form and Bake the Cookies

**4.** *For 9-inch maximonsters:* Using a 7-inch pot lid or round baking pan as a pattern, mark with a fingertip a circle into the greased surface of each foil-covered baking sheet. Measure a level measuring cupful of dough for each cookie (or divide the batch into four equal parts, if you're using all of it for the large ones). With the fingers and heel of your hand or a rubber spatula, pat the dough for each cookie into a neat round inside the marking. (The cookies will be baked one at a time. If you have only one baking sheet, form each cookie on an individual sheet of greased foil, then bake each in turn on the cookie sheet. Be sure the pan has cooled down before reusing it.)

**5.** *For 6-inch monsters:* Measure out a level ⅓-cup measure for each cookie. Place three mounds, spacing them at least 2 inches apart, on each baking sheet covered with greased foil. Flatten them out to a 5-inch diameter with the fingers and palm of your hand or a dampened rubber spatula.

**6.** *For 3½-inch cookies:* Drop rounded tablespoons of dough onto the greased baking sheet, placing them well apart so there will be about 3 inches of expansion room between them. Flatten the mounds slightly with the palm and fingers of your hand or with a dampened rubber spatula.

**7.** Bake the cookies, regardless of size, in the center of the preheated oven for about 15 minutes, or until they are browning lightly around the edges and the centers are semifirm when lightly touched. The larger cookies should be cooled on the foil, first for 5 minutes on the baking sheet, then on a rack. Cool the small cookies on the baking sheet for 5 minutes, then remove them to a wire rack and cool them completely.

**8.** Bagged, wrapped, or kept in covered containers, the cookies will keep for as long as two weeks at room temperature. The biggest ones should be backed by a round of thin cardboard or two layers of heavy-duty foil as insurance against breakage. For longer storage, refrigerate or freeze them. Refresh them in a 300°F oven for 10 minutes, then cool them again before serving.

*Makes 4 maximonster cookies about 9 inches in diameter; or 12 to 14 6-inch monster cookies; or about 3 dozen 3½-inch cookies*

# TOASTED
## OAT AND RAISIN
# COOKIES

High on anybody's list of comforting foods, oatmeal cookies are predictably popular at bazaars and other fund-raisers featuring good things to eat. Toasting the oats before adding them to the dough is rewarding when you're making these; besides enhancing their oatiness, it adds crunch. On the other hand, if there is no time to be lost in getting sustenance into the hands of the cookie-deprived, you can skip that step.

2½ cups regular (not quick-cooking) rolled oats, toasted (optional)
¾ cup vegetable shortening
¾ cup (packed) dark brown sugar
¾ cup granulated sugar
2 eggs
1 teaspoon vanilla extract
1½ cups all-purpose or whole-wheat flour
1 teaspoon baking soda
1 teaspoon baking powder
1 teaspoon salt
2 teaspoons ground cinnamon
1 teaspoon ground allspice
1½ cups dark raisins

**1.** Preheat the oven to 325°F, with an oven rack in the center position.

**2.** Spread the oats on a baking sheet or a jelly-roll pan and toast them for 15 minutes, stirring them frequently, until they are pale gold and smell deliciously nutty. Reset the oven control to 350°F. Let the oats cool.

**3.** In a mixing bowl (using a wooden spoon) or in the large bowl of an electric mixer, cream the shortening until it is soft. Then beat in, in turn, the brown sugar and the granulated sugar, beating after each addition until the mixture is fluffy. Beat in the eggs and the vanilla.

**4.** Sift together the flour, baking soda,

baking powder, salt, cinnamon, and all-spice. Stir the flour mixture into the creamed mixture. Stir in the cooled oats and the raisins and mix well.

## Form and Bake the Cookies

**5.** *To make 6-inch monsters:* Use a ⅓-cup measure as a scoop and level the top of the dough. Place the mound of dough on a greased baking sheet and flatten it slightly with the palm of your hand to about 5 inches in diameter. Repeat with the remaining dough, leaving at least 2 inches between cookies after flattening. With the flat of a knife blade, push the dough inward to make a neat edge if it has spread unevenly.

**6.** *To make 3½-inch cookies:* Measure dough by rounded measuring table-spoonfuls and place the mounds 3 inches apart on the greased baking sheet; flatten each mound slightly with the palm of your hand.

**7.** Bake the cookies in the center of the preheated oven for 15 minutes (a slightly shorter time for the smaller cookies is likely), until they are firm to the touch and lightly browned around the edges. Cool the cookies on the baking sheet for about 5 minutes, or until they are firm enough to be removed to a wire rack, using a wide metal spatula.

**8.** Allow them to cool completely, then store in a tightly covered container or wrap in aluminum foil or plastic wrap. The cookies will keep for as long as two weeks at room temperature. For longer storage, refrigerate or freeze the cookies. Before serving, refresh them in a 300°F oven for 10 minutes, then cool them again.

*Makes 12 to 14 6-inch monster cookies or 3 dozen 3½-inch cookies*

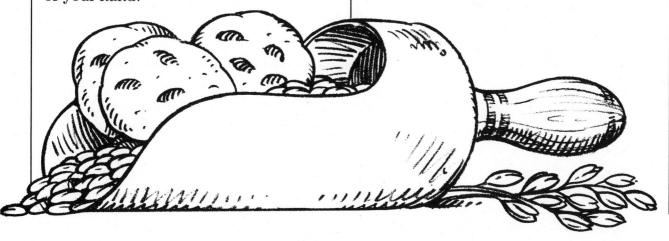

# APPLE SAUCERS

Saucer-size or smaller, spiced, raisined, and rich with apples,

these fruit discs may be left plain or may be glazed. Either way, they're an autumn celebration when the first tart and flavorful apples come to hand.

½ cup vegetable shortening, or ¼ cup vegetable shortening and ¼ cup butter, at room temperature

1¼ cups (packed) light or dark brown sugar

2 eggs

¼ teaspoon lemon extract (optional)

1½ cups all-purpose flour

¾ teaspoon salt

½ teaspoon baking powder

½ teaspoon baking soda

1 teaspoon ground cinnamon

¼ teaspoon ground nutmeg

Big pinch (⅛ teaspoon) ground cloves

1½ cups chopped, peeled, firm tart apples (about 2 medium apples)

1 cup raisins or currants

1 cup regular or quick-cooking rolled oats

1 cup coarsely chopped walnuts

¼ cup apple or orange juice

GLAZE (optional)

1 tablespoon very soft butter

1½ cups sifted confectioners' (10X) sugar

2 to 3 tablespoons apple or orange juice

**1.** Preheat the oven to 350°F, with an oven rack in the center position. Lightly grease a cookie sheet.

**2.** In a mixing bowl (using a wooden spoon) or in the large bowl of an electric mixer, cream the shortening (or shortening and butter) until soft. Then beat in the brown sugar until the mixture is fluffy. Beat in the eggs one at a time, then beat in the lemon extract.

**3.** Sift together the flour, salt, baking powder, baking soda, cinnamon, nutmeg, and cloves. Stir half of the flour mixture into the creamed mixture. Stir in the chopped apples, raisins, oats, and nuts. Stir in the juice, then add and mix in the remaining flour mixture.

### Form and Bake the Cookies

**4.** *For 6-inch monsters:* For each cookie, measure out a level ¼ cup of dough; place the mounds of dough well apart on the greased baking sheet (most sheets will accommodate only three). Flatten the dough, using your fingers or a rubber spatula, to make neat 5-inch rounds.

**5.** *For 2½-inch cookies:* Using a measuring spoon, scoop slightly rounded tablespoonfuls of dough onto the greased baking sheet, spacing them well apart (12 will fit on the average sheet). Flatten the mounds slightly with your fingers or a rubber spatula, and shape their edges neatly, using the flat of a knife blade. For somewhat larger cookies, use a ⅛-cup (2-tablespoon) measure.

**6.** Bake the cookies in the center of the preheated oven for 13 minutes (for smaller cookies) to 15 minutes (average for the 6-inch monsters); they are done when the tops are firm to the touch and lightly browned. Cool the cookies on the sheet, set on a wire rack, for a few minutes, then transfer the cookies to wire racks and cool them completely.

**7.** *Glaze the cookies (optional):* Stir together the soft butter with the confectioners' sugar and 2 to 3 tablespoons of apple or orange juice. While the cookies are still slightly warm, brush this thin icing onto them.

**8.** Store the cookies in snugly covered containers, or in a plastic bag, or wrap in aluminum foil or plastic wrap. They will keep at room temperature for a few days, or they may be refrigerated or frozen for longer storage.

***Makes** about 18 6-inch monster cookies, or 2½ dozen 2½-inch cookies*

# BIG PEANUT HONEYS

Big, bigger, or biggest, these cookies are for fans of peanuts and/or peanut butter, plus anyone who appreciates the taste of honey. Include the raisins as specified, or substitute semisweet chocolate bits, if you like. Why not use butterscotch or peanut butter bits? Candor compels me to say that those on the market, at the time of writing, are not recommendable.

1 cup (2 sticks) unsalted butter or margarine, at room temperature

1 cup chunk-style peanut butter

⅔ cup flavorful honey (avoid bland or delicate honey, such as orange blossom or clover)

1 cup (packed) dark brown sugar

2 eggs

1 teaspoon vanilla extract

2½ cups all-purpose flour

1 teaspoon baking powder

1 teaspoon baking soda

1 teaspoon salt

1⅓ cups raisins

1⅓ cups unsalted roasted peanuts, coarsely chopped (see note below)

**1.** Preheat the oven to 350°F and place an oven rack in the center position.

**2.** In a mixing bowl (using a wooden spoon) or in the large bowl of an electric mixer, cream the butter until it is soft, then beat in the peanut butter until the two are combined. Beat in, in turn, the honey, brown sugar, eggs, and vanilla.

**3.** Sift together the flour, baking powder, baking soda, and salt. Fold the flour mixture into the creamed mixture, then stir in the raisins and chopped peanuts.

## Form and Bake the Cookies

**4.** *To make 9-inch maximonsters:* For each cookie, cover a baking sheet with aluminum foil and grease it lightly. Using a 7- to 8-inch pot lid or round baking pan as a pattern, mark with a fingertip a circle into the greased surface of each foil-covered baking sheet. Measure a level measuring cupful of dough onto the marked foil and pat it out with your hand or a rubber spatula to a neat round inside the marking. Bake the cookie in the center of the preheated oven for 18 to 20 minutes, until it has browned and feels firm when touched lightly near its center. Cool the cookie on the foil, pulled onto a wire rack. (Be sure the sheet has cooled before covering it with foil for the next cookie.)

**5.** *To make 5½-inch monsters:* Scoop up a very slightly mounded ⅓-cup measure of dough for each cookie. Place the dough on an ungreased baking sheet and flatten it with your hand or a rubber spatula to 3½-inch diameter. Repeat, spacing the cookies well apart (three will fit on the average-size baking sheet). Bake the cookies 13 to 15 minutes, or until done as indicated in step 4. Leave the cookies on the sheet for 5 minutes, then lift them off with a metal spatula and cool them on wire racks.

**6.** *For 3-inch cookies:* Measure the dough by rounded measuring tablespoonfuls onto an ungreased baking sheet. Space the mounds of dough well apart and flatten them, with your hand or a rubber spatula, to 2-inch diameter. Bake them 11 to 13 minutes, or until they are done, as described in step 4. Let the cookies cool and firm up on the baking sheet for 5 minutes, then place them on wire racks to cool completely.

**7.** Store the cookies in a tightly closed container at room temperature, or wrap or bag them for refrigerator or freezer storage for a longer period. Before wrapping the largest ones, add a reinforcement to the back, using a round of cardboard or two layers of heavy-duty foil. If the cookies should soften a bit too much, refresh them with 10 minutes in a 300°F oven. Cool them before serving. They can be frozen, and reheated as above (without thawing first) before serving.

*Note:* If salted roasted peanuts are what's available, they can be substituted for unsalted nuts. Rinse them in a sieve under the warm tap, then pat them dry on paper towels before chopping them coarsely.

***Makes** 6 maximonster cookies, about 9 inches in diameter; or 15 6-inch monster cookies; or about 3 dozen 3-inch cookies*

# CHEWY
## MINCEMEAT AND WALNUT COOKIES

¾ cup (1½ sticks) unsalted butter, at room temperature

2 egg yolks

½ teaspoon lemon extract or 1½ teaspoons grated lemon rind, colored outer part only, no pith (optional)

9-ounce package condensed mincemeat, crumbled

⅓ cup coarsely chopped walnuts

1 cup all-purpose flour

½ cup cornstarch

½ cup granulated sugar

½ teaspoon salt

¼ teaspoon ground ginger

¼ teaspoon ground cloves

Substantial, spicy, and full of interesting bits to engage the teeth, these are real cookie-jar cookies—they're at their best after they have mellowed for at least a day. The same is true for the monster size.

**1.** Place an oven rack in the center position and preheat the oven to 325°F for the large cookies and to 350°F if you are making the smaller ones. Grease one or two baking sheets.

**2.** In a mixing bowl (using a wooden spoon) or in the large bowl of an electric mixer, cream the butter until soft, then beat in the egg yolks. Beat in the lemon extract or lemon rind, crumbled mincemeat, and nuts.

**3.** Sift together the flour, cornstarch, sugar, salt, ginger, and cloves. Stir the flour mixture into the creamed mixture to make a stiff dough.

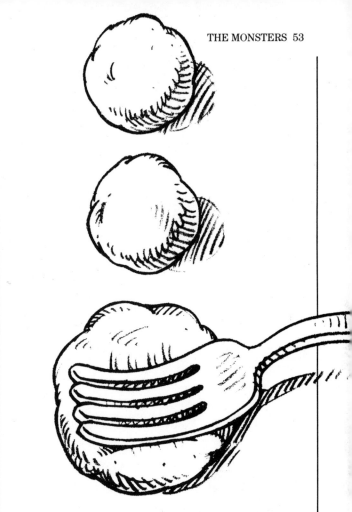

## Form and Bake the Cookies

**4.** *To make 8-inch almost-maximonsters:* Divide the dough in half (about 1⅓ cups per portion). Using a 7½-inch pot lid or round baking pan as a pattern, mark with a fingertip a circle into the greased surface of the baking sheets. Spread one portion of dough evenly, with your hand or a rubber spatula, over each marked circle, leaving the top a little rough (for looks). Bake the cookies one at a time in the center of the preheated 325°F oven for about 25 minutes, or until golden brown and firm. Let the cookie cool on the baking sheet until barely warm, then shift it to a wire rack to cool completely. If you have only one baking sheet, let the sheet cool before forming the next large cookie on it. Shape and bake the remaining dough as described above or make smaller cookies (see step 5).

**5.** *To make 2-inch cookies:* Shape the dough into 1-inch balls and place them 1½ inches apart on a greased baking sheet. Flatten the cookies to about half their thickness, either pressing their centers with the ball of the thumb or making crisscross marks with the tines of a fork dipped into flour. Bake the cookies for about 20 minutes in the center of the preheated 350°F oven until they are golden brown and firm. Cool the cookies completely on wire racks.

**6.** Store the small cookies in an airtight container at room temperature. They can also be refrigerated for up to two weeks, and will last even longer if frozen. The almost-maximonsters should be wrapped in plastic or foil. As insurance against breakage, you may want to add a backing of cardboard or two layers of heavy foil before wrapping them.

***Makes*** *about 2 8-inch monsters; or 3 dozen 2-inch cookies*

# HAZELNUT RAISIN MOUNDS

Rich in the flavor of one of the world's great nuts, rugged-looking but tender to nibble, these mounds are first cousins to "rocks," a traditional American cookie. The dough is especially suitable for making giant cookies, since it doesn't shatter easily after baking. Note, when you're shopping for the nuts, that they are best known as filberts in some regions.

¾ cup vegetable shortening or unsalted butter or margarine, at room temperature

1 cup (packed) dark brown sugar

2 eggs

1 teaspoon maple flavoring

3 cups all-purpose flour

1 teaspoon salt

1 teaspoon baking powder

½ teaspoon baking soda

½ teaspoon ground cinnamon

¼ teaspoon ground nutmeg

4 to 6 tablespoons cold, strong coffee, as needed

1½ cups chopped toasted and skinned hazelnuts (see note below)

1 cup raisins

**1.** Place an oven rack in the center position and preheat the oven to 325°F, if making monster cookies, and to 350°F, for the smaller ones. Grease one or two baking sheets.

**2.** In a mixing bowl (using a wooden spoon) or in the large bowl of an electric mixer, cream the shortening (or butter or margarine) until soft; beat in the sugar and then the eggs. Beat in the maple flavoring.

**3.** Sift together the flour, salt, baking powder, baking soda, cinnamon, and nutmeg. Stir the flour mixture thoroughly into the creamed mixture alternately with 4 tablespoons of the coffee. (The dough should be quite stiff.) Stir in the hazelnuts and raisins. If the dough is too stiff to be pushed easily from the tip of a spoon, add a little more cold coffee, up to 2 tablespoons.

## Form and Bake the Cookies

**4.** *To make 6-inch monsters:* Measure out a generous ¼ cup of the dough for each cookie, using a measuring cup. Flatten each portion of dough on the baking sheet, using your fingers or a rubber spatula, to make a round about 5 inches in diameter. Space the cookies about 2 inches apart on the sheet (most sheets will take only three). Bake the cookies in the preheated 325°F oven about 15 minutes, or until they are firm and golden brown; start checking after 13 minutes. Cool the cookies on the baking sheet for 5 minutes or until firm, then slip them onto wire racks to cool completely.

**5.** *To make 2-inch cookies:* Drop the dough by heaping teaspoonfuls onto the baking sheet, spacing the cookies about 1½ inches apart. Don't flatten the mounds—they should be high. Bake the cookies in the center of the preheated 350°F oven for 13 to 15 minutes, or until they are firm and golden brown. Start checking after 13 minutes. Remove the cookies to wire racks to cool.

**6.** Store the cookies at room temperature in a closed container, or refrigerate them (for up to two weeks) or freeze them for longer storage.

*Note:* To toast and skin hazelnuts, preheat the oven to 325°F. Spread the nuts on a large shallow baking pan and bake them for 20 to 30 minutes, stirring them occasionally, until they smell heavenly and the skins rub off easily. Turn the nuts onto a rough towel, bundle them up, and roll and rub them to loosen as much of the skin as possible. It won't all come off, but that's no problem. Chop the nuts on a board with a big knife or in a blender or food processor, using short on-off bursts of the motor.

***Makes*** *about 15 6-inch monster cookies; or 5 dozen (tall) 2-inch cookies*

# BIG SUGARS

Sugar cookies are ages old and still winners. The sugar may be all white or part brown, as here, and the flavoring may vary from kitchen to kitchen, but these big wheels will probably roll on forever. Fanciers of vanilla cookies may want to replace the nutmeg and lemon rind with a teaspoonful of vanilla extract. This dough can be used for Snickerdoodles (origin of name unknown), which can be any of several types of American cookies. Directions for my favorite are given at the end of the recipe. Sugar cookie dough is also used for maximonster cookies garnished with fruity and nutty oddments to create the dessert "pizzas" on page 42.

*1 cup (2 sticks) unsalted butter, at room temperature*
*1 cup granulated sugar*
*½ cup (packed) light brown sugar*
*2 egg yolks*
*Big pinch (⅛ teaspoon) ground nutmeg*
*1 teaspoon very finely grated lemon rind (colored outer layer only, no pith)*
*2½ cups all-purpose flour*
*2 teaspoons baking powder*
*¾ teaspoon salt*
*About 2 teaspoons water, if needed*
*Coarse or regular granulated sugar, for coating*

**1.** Preheat the oven to 400°F, with an oven rack in the center position. Grease one or two baking sheets lightly.

**2.** In a large mixing bowl (using a wooden spoon) or in the large bowl of an electric mixer, cream the butter until soft. Then gradually add the granulated sugar and the brown sugar and beat until fluffy. Add the egg yolks one at a time, beating well after each addition. Stir in the nutmeg and grated lemon rind.

**3.** Sift together the flour, baking powder, and salt. Stir the flour mixture into the creamed mixture to make a smooth dough. If it seems too dry, add up to 2 teaspoons of water, working it in thoroughly. Form the dough into a ball, wrap it in plastic wrap or aluminum foil, and chill it thoroughly, at least an hour.

## Form and Bake the Cookies

**4.** *To make 7-inch monsters:* For each cookie, measure out a level ⅓ cup of dough. Form the dough into a ball and roll it in regular or coarse granulated sugar. Place the ball on a greased baking sheet and flatten it slightly with your hand, then further with the bottom of a glass pie plate (or a fairly heavy baking pan) dipped into sugar; press until the cookie measures 5½ inches. If the edges have cracked, tidy them by pressing inward around the edge of the cookie with the flat of a knife blade. Form the remaining cookies, keeping at least 3 inches of space between them on the baking sheet. (Most baking sheets will accept only three.) Bake these large cookies in the center of the preheated oven for about 7 to 8 minutes, or until the centers have puffed and fallen and the edges are golden brown.

**5.** *To make 3-inch cookies:* Measure out

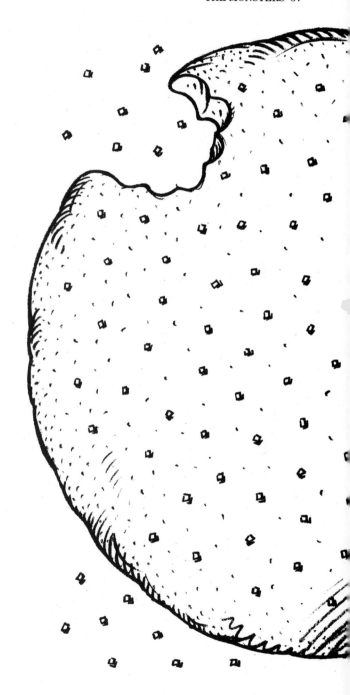

the dough by rounded measuring table-spoonfuls. Form a spoonful of dough into a ball and roll it in regular or coarse granulated sugar. Place the ball on the greased baking sheet and flatten it to 2-inch diameter with the bottom of a metal measuring cup or another flat object, dipped into more sugar if the dough tends to stick. Repeat with the remaining dough, leaving 3 inches between cookies. Bake the cookies in the center of the preheated oven about 6 minutes, or until done as indicated in step 4.

**6.** Cool the cookies on the baking sheet for at least 5 minutes or until they are firm, then lift them off carefully and cool them completely on a wire rack. To store the cookies, pack the smaller ones in a canister or other covered container, not airtight—they'll keep their crispness longer if the cover is a bit loose. Sandwich larger cookies between pieces of heavy-duty aluminum foil or cardboard to prevent breakage and wrap them in foil or plastic wrap. They will keep for as long as two weeks at room temperature. If they should become soft because of humidity, warm them for about 10 minutes in a 300°F oven, then cool them again before serving. The cookies freeze very well; to refresh their flavor and texture, warm them as described above; it isn't necessary to thaw them first.

## Snickerdoodles

To make Snickerdoodles, add a liberal amount of cinnamon, enough to tint it pale brown, to the sugar in which the dough for the smaller Big Sugars is rolled before baking. Bake the Snickerdoodles exactly like Big Sugars.

***Makes*** *about 10 7-inch monster cookies or 3 dozen 3-inch cookies*

# MARVELOUS MEDIUM-SIZE MOUTHFULS

Including Bar Cookies, Chewy Cookies, Brownies, Crisp Cookies, and Gooey Cookies.

# RASPBERRY ALMOND LINZER BARS

In paying cookie homage to the sublime Austrian pastry called *Linzertorte*, I have replaced the fiddly lattice top of the torte with a delicate crust topping of almonds, sugar, butter, and egg. After cutting the whole business into serving pieces, you have raspberry "sandwiches," with cookie pastry as the bottom layer. Despite all the good things that go into them, these are not overly sweet—people have been known to devour them for breakfast.

COOKIE LAYER

¾ cup all-purpose flour

3 tablespoons granulated sugar

½ teaspoon salt

6 tablespoons (¾ stick) unsalted butter, cut up and chilled

2 tablespoons finely chopped, toasted, blanched almonds (see the note following Almond Cookies, page 94)

½ teaspoon almond extract

½ teaspoon vanilla extract

JAM LAYER

⅔ cup thick pure raspberry jam or preserves

TOPPING

3 tablespoons unsalted butter, at room temperature

6 tablespoons confectioners' (10X) sugar, sifted

Pinch of salt

½ cup finely chopped or ground toasted blanched almonds (see the note following Almond Cookies, page 94)

1 egg, lightly beaten

**1.** Preheat the oven to 350°F, with an oven rack in the center position.

**2.** *Make the cookie layer:* In a mixing bowl, whisk together the flour, sugar, and salt. (Alternatively, blend them in a food processor.) Add the butter pieces and cut them in, using a pastry blender or two knives criss-cross fashion if mixing by hand, or by flicking the motor on and off rapidly if a food processor is used. The mixture should have the consistency of cornmeal when the butter has been sufficiently incorporated. Mix in the almonds, almond extract, and the vanilla. You should now have a dough. In the unlikely event that the mixture is too dry to hold together when a sample is squeezed, add only a drop or two of water and mix the dough again.

**3.** *Make the jam layer:* Spread the dough evenly in an ungreased 8-inch square baking pan, pressing it up the sides about ¼ inch to prevent the jam layer from running under the edges of the crust. Spread the raspberry jam over the pastry.

**4.** *Make the topping:* In a mixing bowl (or the food processor), cream the butter until soft. Beat in the confectioners' sugar and the salt until it is fluffy. Then reserve 2 tablespoons of the almonds and mix the rest into the topping. Beat in the egg. Drop the mixture by spoonfuls over the jam layer and spread it lightly without attempting to make the top smooth (it will level during baking). Strew the reserved almonds over the top and knock the pan against the work surface to distribute the chopped nuts evenly.

**5.** Bake the Linzer bars about 30 minutes in the center of the preheated oven; they are done when the top is golden brown. Set the pan on a wire rack to cool. While the panful is still slightly warm, cut it into bars (make 5 vertical cuts and 2 horizontal cuts) or divide the panful into quarters, then cut twice, corner to corner, within each quarter. When the bars are completely cool, remove them carefully. Wrap the bars in aluminum foil or plastic wrap or place them in a covered container. Store the bars at room temperature for a few days, or refrigerate them for longer storage. They also freeze well. If they are to be served from the refrigerator or freezer, allow them to come to room temperature first.

***Makes** 1 8 x 8-inch panful (18 bars, about 1⅓ x 2⅓ inches, or 16 triangles 4 inches long)*

# TOFFEE TOPS

For these confections, a layer of bubbling brown sugar goes over a partly baked cookie-bar base. After a further brief baking, this is topped with chocolate and a finish of chopped almonds. Toffeetops should be served in small pieces.

COOKIE CRUST

*1¼ cups all-purpose flour*

*2 tablespoons (packed) light brown sugar*

*¼ teaspoon salt*

*½ cup (1 stick) unsalted butter, cut up and chilled*

*¼ cup chopped, toasted, blanched almonds (see the note following Almond Cookies, page 94)*

*¼ teaspoon almond extract*

BROWN SUGAR LAYER

*½ cup (packed) light brown sugar*

*⅓ cup (5⅓ tablespoons) unsalted butter*

*1 tablespoon water*

CHOCOLATE TOPPING

*¾ cup (4½ ounces) semisweet chocolate pieces*

*2 tablespoons unsalted butter*

*¾ cup finely chopped, toasted, unblanched almonds (see the note following Almond Cookies, page 94)*

**1.** Preheat the oven to 350°F, with an oven rack in the center position. Grease an 8-inch square baking pan.

**2.** *Make the cookie crust:* Stir together the flour, brown sugar, and salt. Cut in the butter, using a pastry blender, two knives used scissors-fashion, or a food processor (flicking the motor on and off rapidly), until the mixture resembles coarse meal. Stir in the almonds and the almond extract. Press the crumbly dough evenly over the bottom of the pan.

**3.** Bake the cookie crust 12 minutes, until it is slightly firm when pressed lightly. Remove it from the oven.

**4.** *Make the brown sugar layer:* Combine the ½ cup of brown sugar, the butter, and water in a small, heavy saucepan. Bring the mixture to a boil and continue to boil, stirring, for exactly 1 minute. Spread the mixture over the baked cookie base. Return the pan to the oven and bake the topping 10 minutes, or until the brown sugar is bubbling vigorously all over. Remove the pan from the oven to a wire rack to cool for a few minutes.

**5.** *Make the chocolate topping:* Melt the chocolate pieces with the 2 tablespoons of butter in a small, heavy saucepan over very low heat, or in the top of a double boiler over simmering water, stirring constantly. When the brown sugar layer has cooled to become crusty, 5 minutes or more, pour the chocolate topping over it and smooth it out. Sprinkle the chopped unblanched almonds over the chocolate and shake the pan to make an even layer. Press the nuts slightly into the chocolate. Let the panful cool on the rack, and while it is still warm, go around the edges with a knife to loosen the layers from the sides.

**6.** When the Toffeetops are completely cool and the topping has set, cut the panful into small bars, about 1 x 2½ inches, and lift them carefully from the pan. Wrap the bars in aluminum foil or plastic wrap and store at room temperature (for a few days) or in the refrigerator or freezer for longer storage.

***Makes** 1 8 x 8-inch panful (2 dozen bars, 1 x 2½ inches)*

# COCONUT CHOCOLATE AND ALMOND BARS

Layered and rich in good things, these candylike bars are not for the faint of heart when it comes to calories, so they are presented in confection-size portions.

COOKIE CRUST

1⅓ cups all-purpose flour

2 tablespoons (packed) light or dark brown sugar

¼ teaspoon salt

½ cup (1 stick) unsalted butter, cut up and chilled

CANDY TOPPING

½ cup (3 ounces) semisweet chocolate pieces

1 egg

1 cup (packed) light brown sugar

1 tablespoon all-purpose flour

¼ teaspoon salt

⅛ teaspoon almond extract

¾ cup flaked coconut

⅓ cup sliced or coarsely chopped almonds, either blanched or unblanched

**1.** Preheat the oven to 350°F, with an oven rack in the center position. Lightly grease an 8-inch square baking pan.

**2.** *Make the cookie crust:* In a mixing bowl, stir together the flour, brown sugar, and salt. With a pastry blender or two knives used scissors-fashion, cut in the butter just until the mixture is in fine particles that tend to hold together when squeezed. (This may also be done in a food processor by flicking the motor on and off rapidly.) Press the mixture evenly over the bottom of the prepared pan, allowing it to rise very slightly (about ¼ inch) up the sides.

**3.** Bake the cookie crust in the center of the preheated oven for 15 minutes, or until it is moderately firm when it is touched lightly.

**4.** *Make the candy topping:* Remove the pan from the oven (leave the oven on) and scatter the chocolate pieces evenly over the crust and let them melt.

**5.** For the next layer of topping, in a small bowl beat the egg until it is thick and fluffy. Gradually beat in the brown sugar, then beat in the flour, salt, and almond extract. Stir in the coconut, reserving 2 tablespoons, and the almonds.

**6.** Spread the now melted chocolate over the crust with a rubber spatula, then spread the egg mixture over it. Sprinkle the top with the reserved coconut.

**7.** Return the pan to the oven and bake the whole arrangement again for 20 minutes, or until the topping is lightly browned and bubbly. Set the pan on a wire rack to cool completely. While the confection is still slightly warm, cut it into 1 x 2-inch bars.

**8.** Store the bars, wrapped in aluminum foil or plastic wrap or in a covered container, for a day or two at room temperature; refrigerate or freeze them for longer storage. If they are to be served from the refrigerator or freezer, allow them to come to room temperature first.

***Makes** 1 8 x 8-inch panful (24 bars, 1 x 2 inches)*

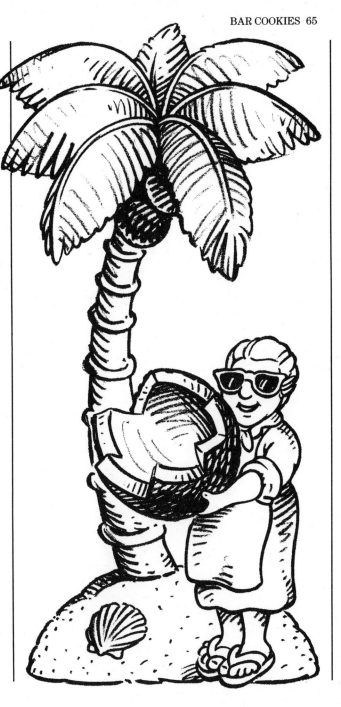

# OAT LACIES

Of a whole Scottish-American collection of flourless macaroon-type cookies made with oats, this is the one I like the best. It isn't essential to toast the oats for these lace cookies, which spread during baking into an openwork pattern with a slickly glazed base, but I do recommend it; the resulting nutty flavor can't be achieved in any other way. (Incidentally, whenever I have time, I toast the oats for other oatmeal cookies, as well.)

*2 cups regular (not quick-cooking) rolled oats*

*1 teaspoon baking powder*

*½ teaspoon salt*

*2 tablespoons unsalted butter, at room temperature*

*1 cup granulated sugar*

*2 eggs, beaten*

*¼ teaspoon almond extract or 1 teaspoon vanilla extract*

**1.** Place an oven rack in the center position and preheat the oven to 325°F, if you're going to toast the oats; otherwise, set it for 350°F. For baking the cookies, cover a baking sheet with aluminum foil and grease the foil lightly.

**2.** *To toast the oats:* Spread them on another large baking sheet or a jelly-roll pan and bake them at 325°F, stirring them often and watching carefully, until they have toasted lightly and evenly, about 15 minutes; they should be a pale gold and smell deliciously nutty. Cool the oats and reset the oven to 350°F.

**3.** Stir together the cooled oats, baking powder, and salt; set aside.

**4.** In a mixing bowl (using a wooden spoon) or in the large bowl of an electric mixer, mix together the butter and sugar until they are completely combined. Stir in the beaten eggs and the almond or vanilla extract thoroughly, then stir in the oat mixture.

**5.** Drop the mixture by heaping teaspoonfuls onto the foil-covered baking sheet, placing them well apart; flatten each mound slightly with a rubber spatula.

**6.** Bake the cookies in the center of the preheated oven for 12 to 14 minutes, until they are golden brown with slightly browner edges; don't overbake them. Slide the foil onto a large wire rack and cool the cookies on the foil. Store the cookies in a covered container at room temperature for a few days, or in the refrigerator or freezer for longer storage. If they should soften during storage in damp weather (or from the refrigerator or freezer), warm them for 5 minutes in a 300°F oven and cool them again before serving.

### Oat and Coconut Lacies

Add ½ cup of flaked coconut to the batter.

### Cinnamon Lacies

Substitute ½ teaspoon of ground cinnamon, mixed with the flour mixture, for the almond or vanilla extract.

***Makes** about 30 3-inch cookies*

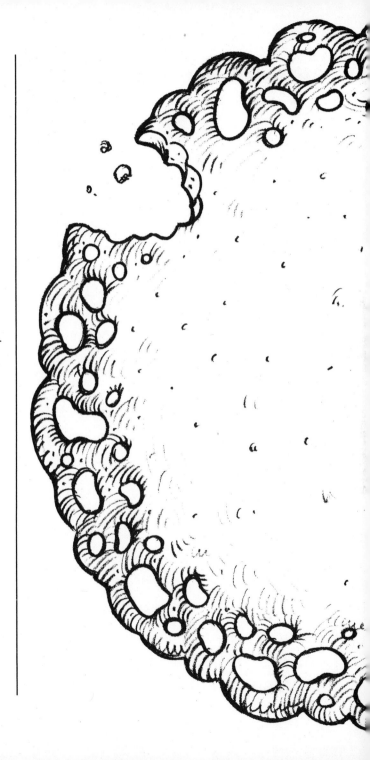

# ALMOND MACAROONS

Chewy, dense, the real thing—macaroons good enough to rate, as an accompaniment, a fine cup of freshly brewed Jamaica Blue Mountain coffee, or your best and rarest tea.

*1 cup blanched almonds*
*½ cup granulated sugar*
*Big pinch of salt*
*Scant ½ teaspoon very finely grated lemon peel (colored outer layer only, no pith)*
*1 egg white, slightly beaten*
*¾ teaspoon almond extract*

GARNISH (optional)
*About 20 halved candied cherries, or squares of candied orange peel, or halved unblanched almonds, or pecan halves (one for each cookie)*

**1.** Preheat the oven to 325°F, with an oven rack in the center position. Cover a baking sheet with aluminum foil.

**2.** Using a nut grater, a food grinder, a food processor, or a blender, grind the almonds very fine. (Do this in two or more batches, if you're using a blender, to prevent the ground nuts from gathering in oily clumps.)

**3.** In a mixing bowl or the container of a food processor (don't attempt this step with a blender), combine the ground almonds, sugar, salt, and lemon peel and work them together thoroughly (stir vigorously with a wooden spoon if you're doing this by hand; a food processor requires a few short on-off bursts of the motor). Starting with about half of the beaten egg white, work it in thoroughly, using a spoon. Add more of the white until you have a grainy paste thick enough to stand up sturdily in a spoon; use all of the egg white, if the mixture will accept it without becoming too moist. Work in the almond extract.

**4.** Form macaroons, either by pushing a heaped teaspoonful of the mixture from the spoon with another spoon, or by rolling teaspoonfuls into balls with your hands, or by using a pastry bag fitted with a large star tube. Shape the macaroons on the foil-covered baking sheet, leaving about 1 inch between them.

**5.** For the optional garnish: Press a candied cherry half, or a square of orange peel, or a nut half into the top of each.

**6.** Bake the macaroons in the center of the preheated oven for about 15 minutes, until they are just golden and barely firm, not browned; you don't want to overbake them lest they become hard (see note below). Slip the foil off the sheet and let the macaroons cool on it for a few minutes, then loosen them by peeling the foil away. Place the macaroons on a wire rack to cool completely, then store them at room temperature in a closely covered container for a few days. For longer keeping—up to several weeks—refrigerate them, suitably wrapped.

*Note:* Macaroons that have been baked to hardness can be salvaged. Cool them as described, then enclose them in a tightly covered container with half of an apple. Check the cookies after a day or two—they should be nicely chewy. Discard the apple at this point.

***Makes*** *about 20 2-inch cookies*

# HAZEL NUT MACAROONS

Hazelnuts (or filberts) are the caviar of nuts, the epitome of nuttiness, rich yet delicate. Their qualities are celebrated in this recipe for a classic macaroon made with only four ingredients, counting the pinch of salt. A slightly fancier version includes the optional chopped candied cherries. A dusting of confectioners' sugar is an attractive finish for macaroons both plain and fancy.

*1½ cups shelled hazelnuts, toasted and skinned (see Hazelnut-Raisin Mounds, page 54)*

*1 cup granulated sugar*

*Big pinch (⅛ teaspoon) salt*

*2 egg whites*

*¼ cup finely chopped candied cherries (optional)*

GARNISH (optional)

*About 12 candied cherries, halved; or confectioners' (10X) sugar, for dusting*

**1.** Preheat the oven to 325°F, with an oven rack in the center position. Cover a baking sheet with aluminum foil.

**2.** Grind or chop the hazelnuts fine (they should be almost as fine as cornmeal), using a nut grater, a food grinder, a food processor, or a blender. (If you use the blender, grind the nuts in three or more batches to prevent their gathering in oily clumps.)

**3.** In a mixing bowl or the container of a food processor (don't attempt this step in a blender), combine the ground nuts, sugar, and salt and mix them well by stirring vigorously with a wooden spoon (or use a few short on-off bursts of the processor motor). Add the egg whites in three batches, stirring the mixture well or processing it briefly after each addition. You should then have a heavy paste that will hold its form when pinched into a peak between the fingers. If you're adding the candied cherries, stir them in thoroughly at this point.

**4.** Shape the macaroons on the foil-covered baking sheet. If you possess a pastry bag, fit it with a large star tip, fill it with the dough, and press out two dozen rosettes, each about 1½ inches in diameter, spacing them about 1½ inches apart on the sheets. To shape the macaroons by hand, scoop up a heaping teaspoonful of dough for each and either push it onto the foil-covered sheet, using a fingertip or another spoon, or roll it into a ball between your hands. Space the mounds or balls 1½ inches apart. If you are garnishing the cookies with candied cherries, press half a cherry into the top of each. Let the macaroons stand, uncovered, for at least 15 minutes, or for up to an hour.

**5.** Bake the macaroons, one sheet at a time, in the center of the preheated oven for 18 to 20 minutes, or until they have browned lightly and the surface is delicately crusty, not soft, when touched lightly. (Although the dough is dark, you'll be able to judge browning.) Don't overbake (see the note below). Let the macaroons cool on the foil, pulled off the hot baking sheet, for 5 minutes, then carefully peel the foil away from their backs and cool them completely on wire racks. If you wish, sprinkle on confectioners' sugar to coat the cooled macaroons.

**6.** Store the macaroons in an airtight container at room temperature for up to a week, or refrigerate them for longer storage. If you have dusted them with sugar, you may want to add a fresh sprinkling at serving time.

*Note:* If by mischance the macaroons are overbaked to hardness, treat them as recommended in the note following the preceding recipe for Almond Macaroons.

***Makes*** *about 2 dozen 2-inch cookies*

# COCOS
## FROM BRAZIL

In Brazil they've got an awful lot of coconut as well as the coffee in the song, and they like to make quick-as-a-flash cookies from the shredded flesh plus sweetened condensed milk. Cocos are ready to eat in a very few minutes— they're even good warm from the oven—but they keep their toothsomeness for weeks if stored in a cool place.

*3½-ounce can (1⅓ cups) flaked coconut*

*4 to 5 tablespoons sweetened condensed (not evaporated) milk*

*½ teaspoon almond extract*

*½ teaspoon vanilla extract*

GARNISH (optional)

*About 18 candied cherries, or squares of candied orange peel, or halves of almonds or pecans*

**1.** Preheat the oven to 325°F, with an oven rack in the center position. Grease a baking sheet lightly.

**2.** Spread the coconut on a chopping surface and chop it briefly with a few strokes of a big knife or a cleaver, just enough to reduce the particles to about half their original size.

**3.** In a mixing bowl, combine the coconut with 3 tablespoons of the condensed milk. Stir them together thoroughly (a wooden spoon is a good implement), then gradually add another tablespoon of the condensed milk, stirring. Stir in the almond and vanilla extracts. If the mixture (which should be somewhat pasty) requires more of the milk, add it; it should not become wet, but the coconut should hold together readily when a sample of the mixture is squeezed lightly.

**4.** Form the mixture into small loosely packed balls with your fingers, using about a heaping ½-teaspoon measure for each. Place them, as they are formed, about 1 inch apart on the prepared baking sheet.

**5.** *For the garnish (optional):* Press half of a candied cherry, or square of candied peel, or half a nut into the top of each cookie.

**6.** Bake the cookies in the center of the preheated oven for about 10 minutes, until they are golden around the edges and here and there on top; pinch one to see that it has become firm. (Be careful not to bake the cocos too long, or they might become hard.) Cool the cookies on the baking sheet for a few minutes, then lift them off with a spatula and cool them completely on wire racks. Store them in an airtight container at room temperature for up to a few days; for longer storage, refrigerate them.

***Makes*** *about 18 1-inch cookies*

# KISS
# KISSIES

No doubt a Victorian moral could be whistled up for these sweetmeats, which involve innocent-looking coconut kisses enclosing black-hearted but delicious chunks of chocolate, also called kisses (Hershey style). Moral aside, these are easily made and fun to eat. Milk chocolate lovers will want to enclose, in the coconut drops, those classic foil-wrapped chocolate kisses that have a little Hershey's flag waving from the top. For those preferring less-sweet chocolate, use the oversize chocolate pieces (maxichips) now to be found among the baking supplies at the supermarket. These confections are especially delightful when tasted as soon as the coconut kiss has cooled but while the chocolate kiss is still soft.

*3½-ounce can (1⅓ cups) flaked coconut*
*2 egg whites*
*Big pinch (⅛ teaspoon) salt*
*⅓ cup granulated sugar*
*4 to 6 drops almond extract*
*About 18 foil-wrapped milk chocolate kisses, or semisweet chocolate maxichips for baking*

**1.** Preheat the oven to 275°F, with an oven rack in the center position. Grease lightly and flour a baking sheet; set aside.

**2.** *To toast the coconut:* Spread the coconut on a large ungreased baking sheet or jelly-roll pan, fluffing it up and separating any clumps. Place the pan in the preheated oven and toast (or dry) the coconut for 10 to 15 minutes, stirring it once or twice. It should become slightly crisp and may brown slightly, if left long enough. Remove and cool the coconut; leave the oven on.

**3.** While the coconut cools, place the egg whites and salt in the smaller bowl of an electric mixer and beat them at high speed until soft peaks appear when the mixer is lifted. While still beating, add the sugar a teaspoonful at a time, scraping down the sides of the bowl from time to time. When all the sugar has been incorporated, add the almond extract and continue to beat the meringue mixture (which is what this has become) until it forms stiff, unfloppy peaks when the beater is lifted.

**4.** Crush the cooled toasted coconut slightly between your palms and fold it into the meringue, being careful to keep as much air as possible in the mixture.

**5.** Using a measuring teaspoon for scooping and a small rubber spatula (or the tip of a finger) as a pusher, place slightly rounded teaspoonfuls of the mixture on the prepared baking sheet,

spacing them about 2 inches apart. Set an unwrapped chocolate kiss, or a maxi-chip, on each mound of meringue and press it in slightly. Then add a smaller dollop of meringue on top of each cookie to cover the chocolate. If any meringue is left, make additional chocolate-hearted kisses until it has all been used.

**6.** Bake the kisses in the center of the preheated oven for about 30 minutes, until they have taken on a pale tint of gold and feel firm when touched lightly. Cool them on the sheet for 10 minutes, then remove them to wire racks to cool completely. Store the kisses in a closed container at room temperature, or in the refrigerator. If the weather should be humid, they may become slightly chewy; but even if their meringue coating loses its characteristic dryness, they are delicious morsels.

## COCONUT VOLCANOES

These have their chocolate on top rather than inside. To make them, drop small spoonfuls of the meringue mixture on the prepared pan, making them tall rather than wide. Set a semisweet chocolate maxichip, point down, on top of each and push it down slightly. Bake these at 300°F until the cookie surface is dry to the touch and the chocolate has melted a bit, about 25 minutes.

***Makes*** *at least 18 approximately 1½-inch cookies*

# CANDIED
## ORANGE, ALMOND
## AND HONEY
# COOKIES

For the orange component of these soft, slightly chewy cookies, try to find really good candied orange peel—if you can help it, don't use the sorry and near-synthetic candied peel packaged in little plastic tubs for use in holiday baking. In fact, it's well worth your while to make a batch of homemade candied peel, one of the simplest and most satisfactory of sweets. For instructions on how-to, see the accompanying box.

¾ cup (1½ sticks) unsalted butter, at room temperature

¾ cup (packed) light brown sugar

1 egg

2 tablespoons honey

4 tablespoons finely chopped candied orange peel (see the note below)

½ cup coarsely chopped unblanched almonds

2 cups all-purpose flour

½ teaspoon baking soda

½ teaspoon baking powder

¼ teaspoon salt

GARNISH (optional)

Chopped candied orange peel (one pinch per cookie)

Chopped unblanched almonds (one pinch per cookie)

**1.** Preheat the oven to 350°F, with an oven rack in the center position. Grease one or two baking sheets lightly.

**2.** In a mixing bowl (using a wooden spoon) or in the large bowl of an electric mixer, cream the butter until soft. Gradually beat in the sugar, then the egg, honey, candied orange peel, and almonds.

**3.** Sift together the flour, baking soda, baking powder, and salt. Stir the flour mixture thoroughly into the creamed mixture.

**4.** Drop the dough by very slightly rounded measuring tablespoonfuls onto the prepared baking sheet, spacing the cookies about 3 inches apart. Flatten each to about half its original height with the tines of a fork, dipped into ice water.

**5.** *For the garnish (optional):* Sprinkle a pinch each of chopped candied peel and chopped almonds on each cookie, if you wish.

**6.** Bake the cookies one sheet at a time in the center of the preheated oven for 10 to 12 minutes, or until they are light golden brown; avoid overbaking them. Cool the cookies on the pan for 5 minutes, then slide them onto wire racks to cool completely. Store them, in a tightly covered container, at room temperature for a few days, or bag or wrap them for longer storage in the refrigerator or freezer. If they should soften too much, perk them up with 5 to 10 minutes in a 300°F oven. Cool them again before serving.

*Note:* If the peel you are using is heavily coated with sugar, rinse the strips under hot water for a moment to remove the excess. Blot the strips dry on paper towels, then chop.

***Makes*** *about 3 dozen 3-inch cookies*

# CANDIED ORANGE PEEL

This keeps well so make a pound or so at a time. You'll need:
*4 large oranges with clear, brilliant skin (preferably navels)*
*2 cups water*
*1½ cups granulated sugar*
*¼ cup light corn syrup*
*Granulated sugar, for coating the peel*

Cut off the top and bottom of each orange, being careful not to cut into the flesh. Score the peel of each into quarters. Using a teaspoon held with its bowl facing toward the fruit, pry off the quarters of peel. Place the peel in a large saucepan and cover it with water; bring to a boil over medium heat. Boil the peel 5 minutes, then drain, return it to the pan, add fresh water to cover, and repeat the whole process. After the second boiling, cut the peel into neat strips, wide or narrow. Then boil the strips again, in fresh water to cover, for 5 minutes, and drain them. Bring the 2 cups of water, the sugar, and the corn syrup to a boil in the same saucepan; boil it vigorously for 3 minutes. Add the peel strips and simmer them, watching their progress carefully, until the syrup has boiled down to a large spoonful or two. Remove the strips with a slotted spoon, draining them as you lift, to a platter or baking pan spread with granulated sugar. Roll the strips in the sugar and let them cool before storing in a covered container at room temperature.

# GLAZED
## SWEET CHOCOLATE AND PECAN BROWNIES

For making these particular brownies, small (4-ounce) bars of sweet chocolate labeled "German's" can be found on the baking supplies shelf of most supermarkets. They have been a staple for many years, especially since some bygone cook developed a pop-ular recipe for German's Sweet Chocolate Cake, still to be found in many recipe collections. If you can't locate the chocolate bars, check a confectioner's shop for dark sweet chocolate in bulk, which does equally well.

½ cup (1 stick) unsalted butter

3 ounces (12 squares) German's sweet chocolate, or 3 ounces of another dark sweet chocolate

2 eggs

1 cup granulated sugar

1 teaspoon vanilla extract

¾ cup all-purpose flour

¼ teaspoon salt

1 cup coarsely chopped pecans

GLAZE

1 ounce (4 squares) German's sweet chocolate, or 1 ounce of another dark sweet chocolate

1 tablespoon unsalted butter

**1.** Preheat the oven to 350°F, with an oven rack in the center position. Grease an 8-inch square baking pan.

**2.** In a small, heavy saucepan over low heat (or in the top of a double boiler over simmering water), melt the butter and chocolate together, stirring constantly. Set it aside to cool.

**3.** In a mixing bowl (using a whisk) or the large bowl of an electric mixer, beat the eggs well, until they begin to thicken. Then beat in the sugar gradually to make a fluffy mixture. Add the vanilla and cooled chocolate mixture and blend them in thoroughly.

**4.** Sift the flour together with the salt. Stir the flour mixture into the creamed mixture, then stir in the pecans. Spread the batter in the prepared pan.

**5.** Bake the brownies in the center of the preheated oven for 25 minutes, or until the center is barely firm when touched lightly. Set the pan on a wire rack to cool.

**6.** *Glaze the warm brownies:* In a small, heavy saucepan over very low heat (or in the top of a double boiler over simmering water), melt the chocolate and butter together, stirring constantly. Drizzle the chocolate mixture over the top of the brownies, then spread it with a rubber spatula. Let the glaze set before cutting the completely cooled brownies into squares or bars.

**7.** The brownies may be stored, covered, in their pan, or wrapped in aluminum foil or plastic wrap or in a plastic bag.

They will keep at room temperature for a few days, or in the refrigerator for up to several weeks. They can also be frozen.

*Makes 1 8 x 8-inch panful (16 2- inch squares)*

## COOKIES AND ICE CREAM

For sudden treats you can spring from the freezer on short notice, several combinations of cookies and ice cream commend themselves.

For a sumptuous dessert, sandwich vanilla ice cream between the halves of split extra-large Glazed Sweet Chocolate and Pecan Brownies (or choose Quick Nutted Brownies, page 86). Wrap each portion snugly in foil or freezer-weight plastic wrap and store them for up to a month in the deep-freeze. Let the filled brownies soften in the refrigerator for a few minutes before serving them with a drizzle of chocolate sauce and/or lightly whipped cream.

For cookie and ice cream sandwiches to enjoy as snacks, use unfilled wafers made according to the recipe for Chocolate-Peppermint Sandwich Cookies, page 102, and fill them with peppermint-candy or vanilla ice cream, then wrap and freeze them. You can do the same with any of the chocolate-chip cookies, which should be baked in flattish rounds about 3 inches in diameter.

# CHOCOLATE-TOPPED PEANUT BUTTER BROWNIES

With the interests of both chocolate and peanut butter fans in mind, these rich bars have been given a double helping of each goody. A little chocolate is swirled enticingly through the crunchy peanut butter batter, and the frosting of more peanut butter is capped with more chocolate, drizzled on and then spanked into little peaks.

¼ cup (½ stick) unsalted butter, at room temperature
¼ cup chunk-style peanut butter
1 cup (packed) light brown sugar
½ cup granulated sugar
2 eggs
1 teaspoon vanilla extract
1½ cups all-purpose flour
1 teaspoon baking powder

CHOCOLATE SWIRL
1½ ounces (1½ squares) semisweet chocolate
2 teaspoons unsalted butter

TOPPING
½ cup chunk-style peanut butter
½ teaspoon vanilla extract
2 tablespoons unsalted butter, melted
1½ ounces (1½ squares) semisweet chocolate

**1.** Preheat the oven to 350°F, with an oven rack in the center position. Grease and flour an 8-inch square baking pan.

**2.** In a mixing bowl (using a wooden spoon) or in the large bowl of an electric mixer, cream the butter until soft. Beat in ¼ cup of peanut butter until they are well combined. Then beat in the brown sugar and granulated sugar in turn, beating well after each addition. Beat in the eggs one at a time, and then add the vanilla.

**3.** Sift together the flour and baking powder. Stir the flour mixture into the creamed mixture, combining them thoroughly. Spread the batter evenly in the prepared pan.

**4.** *Prepare the chocolate swirl:* In a small, heavy saucepan over very low heat (or in the top of a double boiler over simmering water), melt together the chocolate and butter, stirring the mixture constantly until it is smooth. Drizzle the chocolate over the batter, then draw the tip of a knife or a spatula through the chocolate and batter a few times lengthwise and crosswise to swirl them together slightly.

**5.** Bake the brownies in the center of the preheated oven for 30 to 35 minutes, until the top is crusty and the center is barely firm when touched lightly. Set the pan on a wire rack to cool.

**6.** *Prepare the topping:* While the brownies are still slightly warm, stir together the peanut butter, vanilla, and 1 tablespoon of the melted butter (reserve the remainder) until the mixture is spreadable. If it is still quite stiff after stirring, warm it for a minute or so, stirring, in a heavy saucepan over very low heat. Spread the topping over the brownies.

**7.** *Complete the topping:* Place the remaining tablespoon of melted butter and the chocolate in a small, heavy pan over very low heat, or in the top of a double boiler over simmering water, and stir them together until melted and smooth. Drizzle the chocolate in crisscross lines over the peanut butter layer, then "spank" it with the flat of a rubber spatula to make small peaks—the chocolate won't cover the peanut butter completely. Let the topping set before cutting the completely cooled brownies into small bars or squares.

**8.** Store the brownies (covered) in their pan, or wrapped in aluminum foil or plastic wrap, or in a plastic bag. They will keep at room temperature for a few days. For longer storage, refrigerate for several weeks or freeze them.

***Makes*** *1 8 x 8-inch panful (24 brownies, 1 x 2½ inches)*

# PALEFACES: LAYERED BROWNIES

**F**or Palefaces, coconut batter is spooned over a substantial chocolate layer to make split-level bars, pale above and dark below. The three flavors (four, if you count vanilla) make enjoyable harmony in a cookie that's a little off the beaten track for the brownie troop. The same batters can be differently arranged, if you like, to make the Marbled Black and White Brownies a page or two farther along.

½ cup (1 stick) unsalted butter, melted

2 ounces (2 squares) unsweetened chocolate, cut up

¾ cup all-purpose flour

¼ teaspoon salt

2 eggs

1 cup granulated sugar

½ teaspoon vanilla extract

½ cup flaked or grated coconut, coarsely chopped

¼ teaspoon almond extract

½ cup coarsely chopped pecans or walnuts

**1.** Preheat the oven to 350°F, with an oven rack in the center position. Grease an 8-inch square pan.

**2.** Measure 2 tablespoons of the melted butter into a small, heavy saucepan, add the cut-up chocolate, and melt them together over very low heat, stirring until smooth. (They may also be melted in the top of a double boiler over simmering water.) Set aside until the mixture cools.

**3.** Sift together the flour and salt and set aside.

**4.** Beat the eggs in the large bowl of an electric mixer (or in a mixing bowl, using a whisk) until they are thick. Gradually beat in the sugar to make a fluffy mixture; beat in the vanilla, then the remaining melted butter. Fold in the sifted flour mixture by hand, using a wooden spoon or a rubber spatula.

**5.** Measure ¾ cup of the batter into another bowl and stir into it the coconut and almond extract. Set aside.

**6.** Stir the melted chocolate mixture, then the nuts, into the remaining batter.

**7.** Spread the chocolate batter evenly in the prepared baking pan. Drop the coconut batter on top by small spoonfuls, starting with the edges, then spread it out evenly with a rubber spatula.

**8.** Bake the brownies for 25 to 30 minutes in the center of the preheated oven, until the edges have browned very slightly and have begun to draw away from the pan; the center should be firm when touched lightly. Set the pan on a wire rack and cool the brownies completely before cutting them into bars or squares.

**9.** Store the brownies (covered) in their pan, or wrapped in plastic wrap or aluminum foil, or in a plastic bag. The brownies will keep for several days at room temperature. For longer storage, refrigerate them (for up to several weeks), or freeze them.

***Makes** 1 8 x 8-inch panful (16 2-inch squares)*

# MARBLED
## BLACK AND WHITE
# BROWNIES

The two batters used to make Palefaces are simply arranged differently in the pan to create these marbled bars.

*Ingredients for Palefaces (see page 82)*

**1.** Preheat the oven to 350°F, with an oven rack in the center position. Grease an 8-inch square pan.

**2.** Make the batter as described in steps 2 through 4 of the Palefaces recipe. After step 4, divide the batter in half. Stir the melted chocolate mixture and the nuts into one half, and the coconut and the almond extract into the other, as described.

**3.** With the two batters, make a checkerboard pattern as follows: Drop alternating heaping tablespoons of batter into the prepared pan so that there will be a total of two spoonfuls of chocolate and two of coconut in each of four rows, with the mounds placed so that colors alternate horizontally and vertically. Lift the pan a few inches and drop it onto the counter, repeating two or three times, to settle the blobs of batter. With a narrow rubber spatula or a table knife, cut through the batter along each row of ''squares'' in one direction, to swirl the two batters together slightly. Repeat in the rows at right angles to the first cuts. (Don't overdo the swirling—larger blocks of color are more attractive than a mishmash in the finished brownies.)

**4.** Bake the brownies for about 25 minutes in the center of the preheated oven, until the batter has pulled away from the sides of the pan slightly and the top is firm when touched lightly. Cool the brownies in the pan, set on a wire rack. Cut bars of the size you prefer when the cooling is complete. To store the brownies, cover the pan closely with foil or plastic wrap, or remove them from the pan and wrap them snugly, or place them in a plastic bag. They will keep well at room temperature for several days, for several weeks in the refrigerator, or for months in the freezer.

***Makes** 1 8 x 8-inch panful (16 2-inch squares)*

# BLONDE BUTTERSCOTCH BROWNIES

**B**esides the requisite brown sugar and walnuts, we have here a scattering of chocolate chips, if you want to include them. But with or without the chips, these brownies are rich nibbles.

½ cup (1 stick) unsalted butter, at room temperature
¾ cup (packed) light brown sugar
1 egg
1 teaspoon vanilla extract
1 cup all-purpose flour
½ teaspoon baking powder
½ teaspoon salt
¾ cup coarsely chopped walnuts
½ cup (3 ounces) semisweet chocolate pieces (optional)

**1.** Preheat the oven to 350°F, with an oven rack in the center position. Grease an 8-inch square baking pan.

**2.** In a mixing bowl (using a wooden spoon) or in the large bowl of an electric mixer, cream the butter until soft, then beat in the brown sugar, and finally the egg and vanilla. Beat until fluffy.

**3.** Sift together the flour, baking powder, and salt. Stir the flour mixture into the creamed mixture, then stir in the walnuts. Spread the batter in the prepared baking pan. Sprinkle the optional chocolate pieces evenly over the top of the dough and press them down slightly with a rubber spatula.

**4.** Bake the brownies in the center of the preheated oven for 25 to 30 minutes, or until they have begun to pull very slightly away from the sides of the pan. Cool the brownies in the pan, set on a wire rack. Cut the panful into squares or bars when completely cool. The brownies may be stored, covered, in their pan, or wrapped in plastic wrap or aluminum foil, or in a plastic bag. They will keep for several days at room temperature, for up to several weeks in the refrigerator, or even longer in the freezer.

***Makes** 1 8 x 8-inch panful (16 2-inch squares)*

# QUICK NUTTED BROWNIES

The shortest distance between yourself and a panful of brownies is by way of this recipe, a direct-action number that instructs the hungry cook to put everything (well, almost everything) into one bowl, then beat. For the streamlined method, thanks go to a famous New England food expert, the late Beatrice Vaughan. This, by the way, is a brownie of the "cake" school; it's tall in the pan under a crust of both chocolate bits and nuts.

⅓ cup corn oil or other bland vegetable oil (do not *substitute other shortening*)

6 tablespoons unsweetened cocoa, preferably Dutch-process

1 egg

1¼ cups granulated sugar

1⅓ cups all-purpose flour

½ teaspoon baking soda

½ teaspoon salt

1 teaspoon vanilla extract

¾ cup water

¾ cup (4½ ounces) semisweet chocolate pieces

½ cup coarsely chopped walnuts or pecans

**1.** Preheat the oven to 350°F, with an oven rack in the center position. Grease an 8-inch square pan.

**2.** Measure all the ingredients in turn (except the chocolate pieces and the nuts) into the large bowl of an electric mixer or a mixing bowl. Beat at slow speed (if using a mixer) or by hand with a wooden spoon until everything is combined, then beat at medium mixer speed for 1 minute, until the batter is smooth; if you are mixing by hand, be sure to beat the batter well, about 3 minutes.

Scrape the batter into the prepared pan, spreading it evenly. Sprinkle the chocolate bits over the top and press them in slightly with a rubber spatula. Scatter the nuts evenly over the chocolate.

**3.** Bake the brownies in the center of the preheated oven for 35 minutes, or until a cake tester emerges dry from the center. Set the pan on a wire rack and cool the brownies. Cut them into squares or bars when they are completely cool.

**4.** The brownies may be stored, covered, in their pan, or wrapped in plastic wrap or aluminum foil or in a plastic bag. They will keep at room temperature for several days, or they may be refrigerated for several weeks, or frozen for longer storage.

*Makes 1 8 x 8-inch panful (16 2-inch squares)*

# VANILLA SHORTBREAD

Very simple to make and bake, and perfectly delicious. In its traditional round shape, shortbread was possibly the original giant cookie, often imprinted, in its native Scotland, with a pattern of a thistle surrounded by the sun's rays. Most often now, for neat eating, an undecorated round of shortbread is marked into wedges before baking and cut apart afterward. Oblong cakes of shortbread are traditional, too; take your choice of shapes here. The vanilla and almond extracts are a modern touch added to the ancient formula.

½ cup (1 stick) unsalted butter, at room temperature
⅓ cup sifted confectioners' (10X) sugar
½ teaspoon vanilla extract
⅛ teaspoon almond extract
1 cup all-purpose flour
2 tablespoons cornstarch
Big pinch (⅛ teaspoon) salt
Granulated sugar, for sprinkling (optional)

**1.** Preheat oven to 325°F, with an oven rack in the center position.

**2.** In a mixing bowl (using a wooden spoon) or in the large bowl of an electric mixer cream the butter until soft. Add the confectioners' sugar and cream the mixture until it is very fluffy. Beat in the vanilla and almond extracts.

**3.** Sift together the flour, cornstarch, and salt. Work the flour mixture into the creamed mixture just until a somewhat crumbly dough is formed. (When a sample is squeezed lightly it will hold together.)

**4.** *To make shortbread wedges:* Press the dough into an ungreased 9-inch pie pan, smoothing it with your hands into a uniform layer that stops just short of the pan sides. (This is easiest if plastic wrap is laid over the dough before it is smoothed.) With the tines of a table fork, press an ornamental pattern around the edge of the circle. With a sharp knife, mark the dough into 12 wedges, cutting only halfway through it. Then, using the fork again, prick each wedge in two or three places, piercing all the way through the dough.

**5.** *To make shortbread wafers:* Roll the dough out about ¼ inch thick between two sheets of plastic wrap. Remove the upper sheet of plastic and cut the dough into oblongs measuring about 1½ x 2 inches, using a pastry wheel or sharp knife. Lift them onto an ungreased baking sheet, spacing them about 1 inch apart. Gather, roll and cut the trimmings to the same measurements. With a fork, prick entirely through each wafer in two or three places.

**6.** Bake the shortbread, either the round or the wafers, in the center of the pre-heated oven for 30 minutes, or until it is firm to the touch and only pale gold in color—it should not brown if it is to have the correct delicate flavor. Check on its progress after 20 minutes: if there are signs of browning at that point, lower the oven temperature to 300°F and complete the baking. Remove the round pan to a wire rack to cool. If you have baked wafers, slide them onto a wire rack to cool. Sprinkle the shortbread with granulated sugar while it's warm.

**7.** Before the panful of wedges has cooled, go over the markings again with a knife, cutting completely through this time. If the edges have overbrowned at all, trim them while the shortbread is still warm. Remove the wedges from the pan when they are completely cool.

**8.** Store the shortbread, wrapped in plastic wrap or aluminum foil or placed in a closed container, at room temperature for a few days; or refrigerate it for up to several weeks' storage. It may be frozen for longer storage. Shortbread that has been refrigerated or frozen is perked up by being warmed in a 300°F oven for about 10 minutes, then cooled before it is served.

***Makes** a 7-inch round (12 wedges) or about 16 wafers, 2 x 2½ inches*

# CRISP CHOCOLATE SHORTBREAD

In some Scottish circles, anyone who suggested putting chocolate into shortbread would be chased out of town to the sound of execration and bagpipes. Nevertheless, I'm sure chocolate lovers willing to disregard slight inauthenticity will like this shortbread —it's intensely flavored, not too sweet, and delightfully crisp. Any reputable brand of unsweetened cocoa can be used, but if Dutch-process cocoa is available, do use it. Although this kind of cocoa is quite dark, in flavor it is milder and mellower than cocoas that haven't been "Dutched."

½ cup (1 stick) unsalted butter, at room temperature

½ cup confectioners' (10X) sugar

3 tablespoons unsweetened cocoa, preferably Dutch-process

½ teaspoon vanilla extract

¾ cup all-purpose flour

1 tablespoon cornstarch

Big pinch (⅛ teaspoon) salt

Granulated sugar, for sprinkling (optional)

**1.** Preheat the oven to 325°F, with an oven rack in the center position.

**2.** In a mixing bowl (using a wooden spoon) or in the large bowl of an electric mixer, cream the butter until soft.

**3.** Sift together the confectioners' sugar and cocoa. Beat the mixture into the creamed butter, then beat in the vanilla extract.

**4.** Sift together the flour, cornstarch, and salt. Work the dry ingredients thoroughly into the creamed mixture just until a somewhat crumbly dough is formed. (When a sample of the dough is squeezed lightly it will hold together.)

**5.** *To make shortbread wedges:* Press the dough into an ungreased 9-inch pie pan, smoothing it with your hands into a uniform round that stops just short of the pan sides. (This is easiest to do if a sheet of plastic wrap is laid over the dough before it is smoothed.) With the tines of a table fork, press an ornamental pattern all around the edge of the circle. With a sharp knife, mark the dough into 12 wedges, cutting only halfway through it. Then, using the fork again, prick each wedge in two or three places, piercing all the way through.

**6.** Bake the round pan of shortbread in the center of the preheated oven for 30 minutes, or until the shortbread is just firm—check on its progress after 20 minutes. When done the shortbread will be delicately springy when it is touched lightly in the center. Remove the pan to a wire rack to cool. Sprinkle the shortbread with granulated sugar if you'd like a sparkly finish. Before the panful of wedges has cooled, go over the markings with a sharp knife, this time cutting completely through. Remove the shortbread from the pan when it is completely cool.

**7.** *To make shortbread wafers:* Pat or roll out the dough between two sheets of plastic wrap until it is about ¼ inch thick. Remove the upper sheet of plastic wrap and cut the dough into oblongs measuring about 1½ x 2 inches, using a pastry wheel or a very sharp knife, and place them on an ungreased baking sheet about 1 inch apart. Gather, roll, and cut any trimmings to the same measurements. Prick entirely through each wafer in two or three places, using a fork.

**8.** Bake the sheet of wafers just until they are firm, about 15 minutes. Slip the wafers onto a wire rack to cool and sprinkle them with granulated sugar while still warm, if you wish.

**9.** Store the shortbread, wrapped in plastic wrap or aluminum foil, or placed in a closed container, at room temperature for a few days. Refrigerate it for up to several weeks, or freeze it for longer storage. If it is refrigerated or frozen, it will be at its best if it is warmed in a 300°F oven for about 10 minutes, then cooled, before it is served.

***Makes** 1 7-inch round (12 wedges) or about 16 wafers, 2 x 2½ inches*

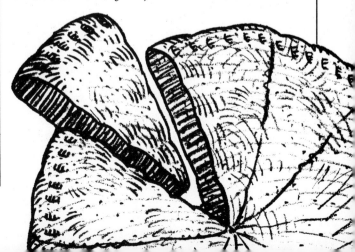

# PECAN SHORTBREAD COOKIES

**P**lain-Jane in looks, anything but plain in flavor if you really and truly appreciate pecans. A sifting of confectioners' sugar is a neat finish, not a gilding of the lily.

*½ cup (1 stick) unsalted butter, at room temperature*
*½ cup confectioners' (10X) sugar, sifted*
*½ teaspoon vanilla extract*
*⅓ cup very finely chopped pecans*
*⅓ cup medium-coarse chopped pecans*
*1 cup all-purpose flour*
*2 tablespoons cornstarch*
*Big pinch (⅛ teaspoon) salt*
*Granulated sugar, for sprinkling (optional)*

**1.** Preheat the oven to 325°F, with an oven rack in the center position.

**2.** In a mixing bowl (using a wooden spoon) or in the large bowl of an electric mixer, cream the butter until soft. Beat in the confectioners' sugar until the mixture is fluffy, then the vanilla. Add all the pecans and mix well.

**3.** Sift together the flour, cornstarch, and salt. Work the flour mixture into the creamed mixture, just until a somewhat crumbly dough is formed. (When a sample is squeezed lightly it will hold together.)

**4.** Spread out a sheet of plastic wrap and heap the dough on it. Cover it with a second sheet of plastic and press the dough to flatten it a bit. With a rolling pin, roll out the dough to ¼-inch thickness. Remove the upper sheet of plastic wrap and, with a pastry wheel or a very sharp knife, cut the dough into oblongs measuring about 1 x 2¾ inches, or any size you prefer. Lift the cookies onto an ungreased cookie sheet, leaving about 1 inch between them. Gather, roll and cut the trimmings to the same measurements. Prick entirely through each cookie in two or three places with a table fork.

**5.** Bake the cookies in the center of the preheated oven for about 15 minutes, until their edges just begin to turn a delicate golden brown and the tops feel firm when touched lightly. Like any shortbread, these cookies should not be overbaked.

**6.** Place the cookies on wire racks to cool. While they are still warm, sprinkle them, if you like, with confectioners' sugar, using a shaker or a small sieve. Store the shortbread, wrapped in plastic wrap or aluminum foil or placed in a closed container, at room temperature for a few days; or refrigerate it for up to several weeks. It also freezes well. If the cookies have been refrigerated or frozen, they will taste best if they are warmed for 10 minutes in a 300°F oven, then cooled, before they are served.

***Makes*** *about 18 wafers, 1¼ x 3 inches*

# ALMOND COOKIES MORE OR LESS CHINESE

The authentic Chinese almond cookie flavor is here, thanks in part to the prodigal amount of almond extract but also to the use of lard, an essential ingredient if you're aiming for the taste that is true. Made medium-size or smaller, these, with their non-traditional crunch of chopped almonds, make a light finish for a meal, and they're just the thing to have with a cup of tea. The well-wrapped dough keeps perfectly in the refrigerator for a few days.

*1 cup lard, or ½ cup lard and ½ cup vegetable shortening, or 1 cup vegetable shortening*

*½ cup (packed) dark brown sugar*

*¼ cup granulated sugar*

*2 eggs, slightly beaten*

*1 tablespoon (repeat—1 tablespoon) almond extract*

*½ cup finely chopped toasted unblanched almonds (see note below)*

*2½ cups all-purpose flour*

*1½ teaspoons baking powder*

*¾ teaspoon salt*

GARNISH

*Whole almonds, either blanched or unblanched, 1 per cookie*

**1.** In a mixing bowl (using a wooden spoon) or in the large bowl of an electric mixer, cream the lard (or lard and shortening, or shortening) until it is soft. Beat in the brown sugar and the granulated sugar until the mixture is fluffy. Measure 2 tablespoons of the beaten egg (reserved for glazing the cookies) and refrigerate it, covered. Then add the remaining beaten eggs, the almond extract, and the chopped almonds to the creamed mixture and mix them thoroughly.

**2.** Sift together the flour, baking powder, and salt. Add the flour mixture to the creamed mixture, blending them thoroughly. Gather this crumbly dough into a ball.

**3.** *Shape and chill dough:* Divide the ball of dough into two equal portions. Place each in the center of a 12-inch length of plastic wrap. If you're making large cookies, shape the dough, with the aid of the plastic rolled around it, into a smooth roll about 2¾ inches in diameter, then flatten the ends. For smaller cookies, make rolls about 1½ inches in diameter, with flattened ends. Close the ends of the wrapping and refrigerate the dough for several hours.

**4.** Preheat the oven to 275°F, with an oven rack in the center position. Add 1 teaspoon water to the reserved beaten egg and mix them well.

**5.** Unwrap a roll of chilled dough and slice it ⅜ inch thick with a serrated knife. Lay the slices 2 inches apart on one or two ungreased baking sheets. Brush the tops of the cookies lightly with the egg glaze and place an almond in the center of each, pushing it slightly into the dough.

**6.** Bake the cookies, one panful at a time, in the preheated oven for 35 to 40 minutes. The cookies are done when they are firm to the touch and the glaze is a rich tawny gold.

**7.** Slide the cookies onto a wire rack and cool them completely. Store them in a covered container at room temperature for up to a week; for longer storage, wrap the cookies, or bag them in plastic, and refrigerate or freeze them.

*Note:* To toast almonds, either blanched or unblanched (natural), spread them on a baking sheet and bake them in a 300°F oven for 10 to 15 minutes, stirring them often. They're done when they smell nutty-toasty and are barely golden (if blanched; unblanched nuts are brown to begin with). In either case, don't overbake them, lest they scorch. Cool the nuts, then chop them on a board, using a sharp, heavy knife, or in a food processor fitted with the steel blade, using quick on-off flicks of the motor switch.

***Makes** 2 dozen 3½-inch cookies, or 3 dozen 2-inch cookies*

# ICED LEMONADE WAFERS

Crisp and cooling, tangy with lemon rind in the cookie and fresh juice in the thin glaze of icing, these are super for summer.

½ cup (1 stick) unsalted butter, at room temperature

1 tablespoon (lightly packed) finely grated lemon rind (colored outer layer only, no pith)

¼ teaspoon almond extract

1 cup all-purpose flour

½ cup confectioners' sugar

1 tablespoon cornstarch

¼ teaspoon salt

ICING

⅔ cup sifted confectioners' (10X) sugar

2 to 2½ teaspoons strained fresh lemon juice

**1.** In a mixing bowl (using a wooden spoon) or in the large bowl of an electric mixer, cream the butter until it is light. Beat in the lemon rind and almond extract.

**2.** Sift together the flour, confectioners' sugar, cornstarch, and salt. Add the flour mixture to the creamed mixture and combine them thoroughly.

**3.** Divide the dough into two equal portions. Roll each portion under your palms on a very lightly floured work surface to form a cylinder 1½ to 1¾ inches in diameter. Flatten the ends neatly, wrap the rolls in plastic wrap, and refrigerate them until the dough is very cold and firm, at least 1 hour. (The dough may be kept for up to a week before it is used.)

**4.** Preheat the oven to 350°F, with an oven rack in the center position. Lightly grease one or two baking sheets.

**5.** Using a serrated knife, slice one or both of the chilled rolls of dough into 16 to 18 slices apiece; the slices should be about ⅛ inch thick. Lay the slices about an inch apart on the baking sheets.

**6.** Bake the cookies one panful at a time in the preheated oven about 8 to 10 minutes, watching them carefully after 6 or 7 minutes and if necessary turning the pan end for end to insure even baking. They are done when the edges are

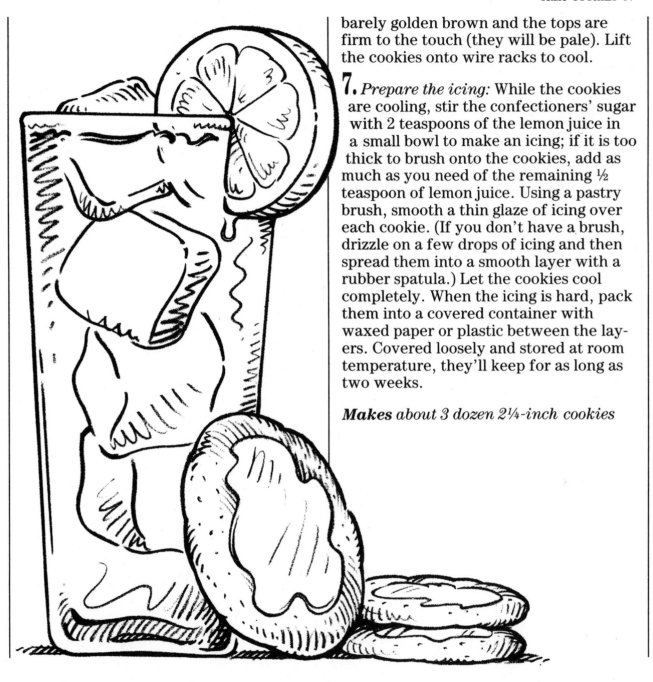

barely golden brown and the tops are firm to the touch (they will be pale). Lift the cookies onto wire racks to cool.

**7.** *Prepare the icing:* While the cookies are cooling, stir the confectioners' sugar with 2 teaspoons of the lemon juice in a small bowl to make an icing; if it is too thick to brush onto the cookies, add as much as you need of the remaining ½ teaspoon of lemon juice. Using a pastry brush, smooth a thin glaze of icing over each cookie. (If you don't have a brush, drizzle on a few drops of icing and then spread them into a smooth layer with a rubber spatula.) Let the cookies cool completely. When the icing is hard, pack them into a covered container with waxed paper or plastic between the layers. Covered loosely and stored at room temperature, they'll keep for as long as two weeks.

***Makes*** *about 3 dozen 2¼-inch cookies*

# SESAME THINS

Here are discs of ultimate nuttiness, thin and crisp, and densely packed with sesame seeds—*the* cookie for people who dote on sesame brittle, that magical mouth-opener among candies.

*2 eggs*
*¾ cup (packed) dark brown sugar*
*½ cup granulated sugar*
*1 tablespoon unsalted butter, melted*
*1 teaspoon vanilla extract*
*¾ cup all-purpose flour*
*½ teaspoon baking powder*
*¼ teaspoon salt*
*⅔ cup hulled white sesame seeds*

**1.** Preheat the oven to 400°F, with an oven rack in the center position. Grease and flour one or two baking sheets.

**2.** In a mixing bowl (using a whisk) or in the large bowl of an electric mixer, beat the eggs until very light. Gradually beat in the brown sugar and granulated sugar. Beat in the melted butter, then the vanilla.

**3.** Sift together the flour, baking powder, and salt. Stir the flour mixture into the egg-sugar mixture, then stir in the sesame seeds.

**4.** Using a measuring teaspoon, scoop up level spoonfuls of batter and drop them onto the prepared baking sheet, leaving about 2 inches between cookies. Bake the cookies one sheet at a time in the preheated oven for 4 to 5½ minutes; the cookies are done when they have bubbled all over and then subsided and have acquired golden brown edges. Cool the cookies for 2 or 3 minutes on the sheet, then transfer them to wire racks to cool completely.

**5.** Store the cookies in a loosely covered container at room temperature for brief keeping, or refrigerate or freeze them for up to a few weeks. If they should lose crispness, refresh them for a few minutes in a preheated low (200°F) oven, then cool again before serving.

***Makes** about 3½ dozen 3-inch cookies*

# TOASTED COCONUTTIES

A crisp and delicious bite just as they come out of the oven, these little cookies are not averse to an edging of apricot preserves that anchor a fringe of more coconut.

*¾ cup (1½ sticks) unsalted butter, at
    room temperature*

*½ teaspoon almond extract*

*1 cup flaked coconut, toasted (see
    Kiss-Kissies, step 2, page 74)*

*1 cup all-purpose flour*

*½ cup cornstarch*

*⅔ cup sifted confectioners' (10X) sugar*

TRIMMING (optional)

*⅓ to ½ cup apricot preserves*

*⅓ cup flaked coconut, toasted (see
    Kiss Kissies, step 2, page 74)*

**1.** Preheat the oven to 300°F, with an oven rack in the center position.

**2.** In a mixing bowl (using a wooden spoon) or in the large bowl of an electric mixer, cream the butter with the almond extract until soft. Beat in the 1 cup of coconut.

**3.** Sift together the flour, cornstarch, and confectioners' sugar. Beat the flour mixture into the creamed mixture. Form the dough into a large ball, wrap it in plastic wrap, and refrigerate it for at least an hour, or until it is firm. (The dough may be refrigerated for up to two days.)

**4.** When firm, remove the dough from the refrigerator, shape it into 1-inch balls, and place them about 1½ inches apart on an ungreased baking sheet. Dip a table fork into flour and flatten each cookie slightly, pressing it once.

**5.** Bake the cookies in the center of the preheated oven until their edges are lightly browned, about 20 minutes. Cool on the sheet about 5 minutes, then remove them to racks to cool completely.

**6.** *Add the optional trimming:* Spread a little of the apricot preserves around the edge of each cookie and sprinkle a little of the additional ⅓ cup of coconut over the jam. Store the cookies in a tightly closed container at room temperature for a few days, or refrigerate them for up to several weeks.

***Makes** 3 dozen 2-inch cookies*

# PECAN PRALINE COOKIES

Close as you can come, in a cookie, to the brown-sugary goodness of the immortal New Orleans praline. When freshly baked the cookies are crisp, and they'll stay that way in dry weather. With a humid turn, though, they become chewy, and I think I like them even better that way.

2 eggs

1¼ cups (packed) dark brown sugar

¼ cup granulated sugar

2 tablespoons unsalted butter, melted

½ teaspoon maple flavoring (or substitute 1 teaspoon vanilla extract)

⅓ cup all-purpose flour

½ teaspoon baking powder

¼ teaspoon salt

1½ cups medium-coarse chopped pecans

**1.** Preheat the oven to 400°F, with an oven rack in the center position. Grease and flour one or two baking sheets.

**2.** In a mixing bowl (using a whisk) or in the large bowl of an electric mixer, beat the eggs until they are light. Gradually beat in the brown sugar, then the granulated sugar; beat well. Beat in the melted butter and the maple flavoring or vanilla.

**3.** Sift together the flour, baking powder, and salt. Stir the flour mixture into the egg mixture. Stir in the chopped pecans. Scoop up level measuring teaspoonfuls of the batter and drop them onto the prepared baking sheets, leaving at least 3 inches between cookies (these spread a lot). Bake the cookies one sheet at a time for 4 to 5 minutes in the center of the preheated oven, until they have turned golden brown (don't overbake them). Leave the cookies on the sheet

## EASY LIFT-OFF

If certain very thin cookies, such as the Pecan Praline Cookies, are left on the pan too long after they come from the oven, they may cling grimly to the metal. The strategy for unsticking them is simple: Return the pan to the hot oven for a moment (watch it carefully), just until the metal is well heated. This will soften the cookies enough to let you lift them off without casualties.

for a minute or two (not too long, or they'll be hard to remove), then transfer them to wire racks to cool completely.

**4.** Store the cookies in a covered container at room temperature for up to a week. They will soften a bit unless the atmosphere is very dry; if you wish to re-crisp them, place the cookies in a warm oven (150°F to 200°F) for a few minutes, then cool them again before serving.

***Makes*** *about 3½ dozen 3½-inch cookies*

# CHOCOLATE PEPPERMINT
## SANDWICH COOKIES

**M**ore addictive than Oreos, these are confected by sandwiching crisp chocolate wafers with either peppermint buttercream or a butterless peppermint filling based on egg white. The secret of making the cookies sufficiently thin is an easily improvised mold that bypasses the problem of cutting very thin slices from a free-form roll of dough. For this recipe, two cans of the size used for Campbell's condensed soups are just right. Be sure that the top and bottom have been taken off smoothly, with no snags, and dry the well-washed cans thoroughly before using them.

*3 squares (3 ounces) unsweetened chocolate, cut up*
*6 tablespoons (¾ stick) unsalted butter*
*¼ cup vegetable shortening*
*¾ cup granulated sugar*
*1 egg, well beaten*
*3 tablespoons water*
*1 teaspoon vanilla extract*
*1¼ cups all-purpose flour*
*1 teaspoon baking powder*
*½ teaspoon salt*
*Peppermint Buttercream or Peppermint Filling (see following recipes)*

**1.** In a small, heavy saucepan over very low heat (or in the top of a double boiler over simmering water), melt the chocolate with 2 tablespoons of the butter, stirring constantly; set aside to cool.

**2.** In a mixing bowl (using a wooden spoon) or in the large bowl of an electric mixer, cream the remaining 4 tablespoons of butter and the shortening together until soft. Beat in the sugar, then beat in, one ingredient at a time, the egg, the water, the melted chocolate mixture, and the vanilla. Beat until well blended.

**3.** Sift together the flour, baking powder, and salt. Stir the flour mixture thoroughly into the creamed mixture.

**4.** Pack the dough firmly into two soup (or other) cans, 2⅝ inches in diameter, whose tops have been smoothly removed. Cover the open end of each can with plastic wrap or aluminum foil and refrigerate the dough for several hours, until it is very firm.

**5.** Preheat the oven to 350°F, with an oven rack in the center position.

**6.** Using a can opener that makes a completely smooth cut, cut around the bottom of each dough-filled can, leaving the bottom disc in place to serve as a pusher. Refrigerate one mold again while you slice the other. Push a very thin portion of dough out of the can and slice it off with a thin, sharp knife; try for cookies 1/16 inch thick. Carefully lay the slice on an ungreased baking sheet. Repeat until the sheet is full, leaving 1½ inches between the cookies.

**7.** Bake the cookies in the preheated oven for 12 to 14 minutes, or until they

are barely firm when touched lightly in the center; do not overbake them. Cool the cookies on the sheet for a few moments, then place them on wire racks to cool completely.

**8.** Make the filling of your choice (see the recipes below). Lay out half of the cookies bottom side up. Spread them generously with filling, leaving a narrow rim clear, then place another cookie, bottom side down, over the filling. Press gently to force the filling just to the edge of the sandwich cookie.

**9.** Let the filling set before serving the cookies or storing them in a covered container. They keep at room temperature for a few days, or in the refrigerator for up to several weeks. The texture becomes softer with storage in humid weather, but either crisp or mellow, the sandwiches are hard to resist.

***Makes*** *about 18 sandwiches, or 3 dozen wafers about 3 inches in diameter*

## PEPPERMINT BUTTERCREAM FILLING

*¼ cup (½ stick) unsalted butter*
*2 cups sifted confectioners' (10X) sugar*
*¼ teaspoon peppermint extract*

Cream the butter until soft. Beat in the confectioners' sugar and beat well until fluffy. Then beat in the peppermint extract. If the icing seems too stiff, add milk or cream cautiously, a drop or two at a time, until the consistency is right for spreading. Check the flavor and add an additional drop or two of peppermint extract if you'd like more mintiness, but be careful not to overdo it.

## PEPPERMINT FILLING

This makes an almost crisp layer after it has "set" between the cookies; it's quite different in texture from the buttercream above.

*2 egg whites*
*¾ cup sifted confectioners' (10X) sugar*
*¼ teaspoon peppermint extract*

Combine the egg whites and confectioners' sugar in the top of a double boiler or a small metal bowl and set the container over, not in, simmering water. Whisk the mixture vigorously, or beat it constantly with a rotary or electric beater, until the filling is thick and warm (not hot) when poked with a fingertip. When ready, it should form fairly stiff peaks when the beater is lifted. Beat in the peppermint extract. Remove the top of the double boiler or bowl from the hot water and beat the filling a minute or two longer. Check the flavor and add another drop or two of extract if it's needed, but be cautious—this essence is powerful, and the filling should enhance, not overwhelm, the flavor of chocolate.

# MACAROON FLATS

Crisp rather than chewy, thin and flat rather than mounded, Macaroon Flats are made from a batter devised to spread during baking.

¾ cup blanched almonds

½ cup granulated sugar

Pinch of salt

Scant ½ teaspoon very finely grated lemon peel (colored outer layer only, no pith)

1 egg white, slightly beaten

¾ teaspoon almond extract

Granulated sugar, for sprinkling

**1.** Preheat the oven to 325°F, with an oven rack in the center position. Cover a baking sheet with aluminum foil.

**2.** Using a nut grater, a food grinder, a food processor, or a blender, grind the almonds very fine. (If you use a blender, do this in two or more batches to prevent the nuts from becoming oily and/or clumping as they are ground.)

**3.** In a mixing bowl or the container of the food processor (don't attempt this step in a blender), combine the ground nuts, sugar, salt, and lemon peel, mixing them thoroughly. (Stir vigorously with a wooden spoon if you're doing this by hand; a food processor requires a few on-off bursts.) Add the egg white and the almond extract and work it in well.

**4.** Form cookies by measuring slightly rounded teaspoonfuls of the batter and placing them on the foil-covered baking sheet about 2 inches apart. Sprinkle the cookies lightly with additional sugar.

**5.** Bake the cookies in the center of the preheated oven for about 15 minutes, until they have spread, flattened, and turned a light gold. Remove the foil from the baking sheet and cool the cookies on it for a few minutes, then cool them completely on wire racks. Store the cookies in a closed container at room temperature for a few days, or freeze them for longer storage. If at any time they should lose crispness, refresh them for a few minutes in a preheated 300°F oven. Cool again before serving.

***Makes*** *about 2 dozen 2-inch cookies*

# JAM-TART COOKIES

**F**or filling these crisp tart-shell cookies, choose jams that are full of chunky fruit, not oversweetened and artificially stiffened with added pectin. Good flavor bets are strawberry, raspberry, cherry, apricot, and pineapple preserves. Assorted fillings will turn a plateful of cookies into a colorful dessert; garnish it with a few green leaves for an especially fresh and festive look.

### TART-SHELL COOKIE DOUGH

½ cup (1 stick) unsalted butter, at room temperature

½ cup confectioners' (10X) sugar, sifted

1 egg yolk

½ teaspoon vanilla extract

1½ cups all-purpose flour

¼ cup cornstarch

¼ teaspoon salt

1 to 2 teaspoons strained fresh lemon juice, as needed

### FILLING

About 1 cup (total) thick jam or preserves (all one kind or assorted flavors)

**1.** Preheat the oven to 375°F, with an oven rack in the center position. Cut two 12 x 16-inch sheets of aluminum foil into 24 squares measuring 4 x 4 inches each. Set aside.

**2.** *Make the cookie dough:* In a mixing bowl (using a wooden spoon) or in the large bowl of an electric mixer, cream the butter until soft. Add the confectioners' sugar and beat until fluffy. Beat in the egg yolk and the vanilla.

**3.** Sift together the flour, cornstarch, and salt. Add the flour mixture to the creamed mixture and combine thoroughly. While mixing, sprinkle in 1 teaspoon of the lemon juice. If the dough seems too crumbly add up to 1 teaspoon more juice. Form the dough into a ball, then divide it into two equal portions.

**4.** One portion at a time, roll the dough out ⅛ inch thick between two sheets of plastic wrap. Peel off the upper sheet and cut the dough into rounds with a 2¾-inch cookie or biscuit cutter, preferably one with a fluted edge. Then gather the scraps and reroll them between the sheets of plastic wrap to make more shells. You should have 24.

**5.** *To shape tart-shell cookies:* Place a round of dough in the center of a foil square. Dip the base of a small jar (spice-jar size, 1½ inches in diameter) into flour and set it exactly in the center of the pastry. Upend the whole assembly in one hand and with the other press the foil and pastry gently over the bottom and up the sides of the jar—don't squeeze. Press the foil extending beyond the pastry closely to the jar. Turn over again, remove the jar, and set the shell, in its mold, on a baking sheet. Adjust the shell, if necessary, to be sure its bottom sits flat and the sides are reasonably symmetrical. Repeat with the remaining rounds, placing the shells 2 inches apart.

**6.** Bake the cookies, one sheet at a time, in the center of the preheated oven for about 12 minutes, or until the pastry is golden brown. Slip the foil cups onto a wire rack and cool the shells completely, then remove the foil.

**7.** *Add the filling:* At any time within several hours of serving, spoon about a teaspoonful of jam into each shell and spread it neatly. Any leftover filled cookies may be refrigerated, wrapped in aluminum foil or plastic wrap. The shells will be less crisp, but their mellower texture is still attractive. Unfilled shells will keep, in a covered container in the refrigerator, for a week or more. They may be frozen for longer storage. (Before using either chilled or frozen shells, refresh them for about 10 minutes in a preheated 275°F oven, then allow them to cool again.)

*Makes 2 dozen 2-inch cookies*

## JAM SESSION

For Raspberry-Almond Linzer Bars (page 60), Toasted Coconutties (page 99), and Jam-Tart Cookies (page 106), the jam or preserves you use should be of the best quality. (*Jam,* by definition, is dense and full of small bits of fruit, whereas *preserves* contain larger chunks of fruit suspended in a thick, sometimes jellied, syrup.) If the jam or preserves you have should seem a bit oversoft, boil either in a small saucepan for a minute or two, watching constantly; this will drive off some of the moisture. Cool before use.

# PECAN PIE SQUARES

Cut into small squares, this panful of tender cookie crust with a classic pecan pie filling is finger food; cut into larger pieces and topped with lightly whipped cream, it's dessert. Either way, the recipe is a quick squaring of the pie circle, with a no-roll crust. Blissful eating for pecan people.

COOKIE CRUST

1¼ cups all-purpose flour
¼ cup (packed) light brown sugar
Pinch of salt
6 tablespoons (¾ stick) unsalted butter, cut up and chilled

PECAN TOPPING

1 egg
1 egg yolk
⅓ cup (packed) light brown sugar
½ cup dark corn syrup
¼ teaspoon salt
¾ teaspoon vanilla extract
1½ tablespoons melted unsalted butter
¾ cup coarsely chopped pecans

1. Preheat the oven to 350°F, with an oven rack in the center position.

2. *Make the cookie crust:* In a mixing bowl, combine the flour, ¼ cup light brown sugar, the salt, and the chilled butter pieces. With a pastry blender or two knives used scissors-fashion (or in the food processor, flicking the motor on and off rapidly), cut in the butter until the mixture is like cornmeal; it should hold together when a sample is squeezed. Press the crust mixture evenly over the bottom and ¼ inch up the sides of an ungreased 8-inch or 9-inch square baking pan.

3. Bake the crust in the center of the preheated oven for 10 minutes. Remove the crust from the oven; leave the oven turned on.

4. *Make the pecan topping:* In a mixing bowl, beat or whisk the egg and egg yolk together thoroughly. Add the brown sugar, corn syrup, salt, and vanilla and

whisk or stir until the sugar has dissolved. Stir in the melted butter. Pour the filling into the partly baked crust and scatter the pecans evenly over the top.

**5.** Bake the panful for 20 to 25 minutes in the preheated oven, until the top is firm and slightly browned and the center no longer jiggles if the pan is shaken gently.

Cool the pan on a wire rack. Cut the "pie" into squares when cold, or just before serving. Wrap the squares in plastic or foil, or place them in a covered container, and store in the refrigerator for up to a week. Let them come to room temperature before serving.

*Makes 1 8 x 8-inch or 9 x 9-inch panful (about 16 approximately 2-inch squares)*

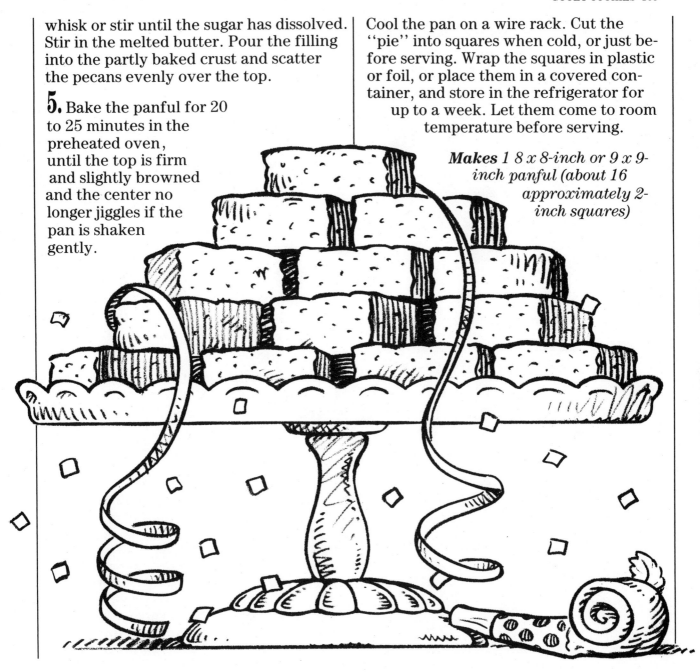

# SLIGHTLY RUMMY PECAN PIE COOKIES

If there's no rum in the cupboard, that item can be omitted from the filling of these miniature nut pies; however, it does add a subliminal something to the combination of pecans and brown sugar. If you delete the rum, increase the vanilla to ½ teaspoon, a better strategy than using artificial rum flavorings.

## COOKIE DOUGH

½ cup (1 stick) unsalted butter, at room temperature
½ cup confectioners' (10X) sugar, sifted
1 egg yolk
½ teaspoon vanilla extract
1½ cups all-purpose flour
¼ cup cornstarch
¼ teaspoon salt
1 to 2 teaspoons strained fresh lemon juice, as needed

## PECAN FILLING

⅓ to ½ cup coarsely chopped pecans
1 egg
⅓ cup (packed) light brown sugar
2 tablespoons light corn syrup
Pinch of salt
1 tablespoon dark Jamaica rum (or medium or light rum)
¼ teaspoon vanilla extract
1½ tablespoons melted unsalted butter

**1.** Preheat the oven to 350°F, with an oven rack in the center position. Cut two 12 x 16-inch sheets of aluminum foil. Cut the foil into 24 squares measuring 4 x 4 inches each. Set them aside.

**2.** *Make the cookie dough:* In a mixing bowl (using a wooden spoon) or in the large bowl of an electric mixer, cream the butter until soft. Add the confectioners' sugar and beat the mixture until it is fluffy. Beat in the egg yolk and the vanilla.

**3.** Sift together the flour, cornstarch, and salt. Add the flour mixture to the creamed mixture and combine thoroughly. While mixing, sprinkle in 1 teaspoon of the lemon juice. If the dough seems too crumbly to hold together, add up to 1 teaspoon more juice. Form the dough into a ball, then divide it into two equal portions.

**4.** One portion at a time, roll the dough out ⅛ inch thick between two sheets of plastic wrap. Peel off the upper sheet and cut the dough into rounds with a 2¾-inch cookie or biscuit cutter, preferably one with a fluted edge. Then gather the scraps and reroll them between the plastic sheets to make more shells. Each portion of dough will make 12 shells.

**5.** *To shape pie-shell cookies:* Place a round of dough in the center of a foil square. Dip the base of a small jar (spice jar size, 1½ inches in diameter) into flour and set it carefully in the center of the pastry. Upend the whole business in one hand and with the other press the foil and pastry gently over the bottom and up the sides of the jar—don't squeeze. Press the foil extending above the pastry closely to the jar. Turn everything over again, remove the jar, and set the shell, in its mold, on a baking sheet. Adjust the shell, if necessary; be sure its bottom sits flat and the sides are reasonably symmetrical. Repeat with the remaining rounds, placing the shells about 2 inches apart, until all the dough has been used. (This is fairly quick to do and fairly complicated to explain.)

**6.** *Make the filling:* Divide the pecans among the pastry cups, placing a scant teaspoonful in each. Beat together the egg, brown sugar, corn syrup, salt, rum, and vanilla until the sugar has dissolved. Stir in the melted butter. Pour the filling carefully over the nuts in the shells, using a teaspoon; divide the filling equally among them, about a teaspoonful per pie.

**7.** One sheet at a time, bake the cookies in the center of the preheated oven for about 20 minutes, or until the pastry is golden and firm; don't let it overbrown. While baking, the filling will boil up a bit and may even overflow once in a dozen cookies, but no harm's done. Cool the pielets in their foil shells, and serve them fresh. If there are leftovers, they're still very good to eat after a day or two of refrigeration. Wrap them well or place them in a covered container, and refrigerate.

**Makes** *2 dozen 2-inch cookies*

# PEANUT BUTTER AND JELLY PILLOWS

As any connoisseur of childhood delicacies knows, the combination of fillings in these cushiony cookies is an all-time great. Concord grape jelly is traditional in children's peanut butter sandwiches, but because jelly tends to melt inside the cookies during baking, Concord grape jam, which is more stalwart, is called for here. (The jam is stocked by most supermarkets; be sure to buy a brand made with fruit and sugar only, no pectin, to get a desirably dense consistency.) Baking done, the cook who makes these can hark back happily to kidhood—a crunchy-crumbly, jelly-hearted cookie in one hand, a glass of cold milk (what else?) in the other.

COOKIE DOUGH

*1 ½ cups all-purpose flour*

*½ cup granulated sugar*

*½ teaspoon baking soda*

*¼ teaspoon salt*

*⅓ cup (5⅓ tablespoons) unsalted butter or margarine, cut up and chilled*

*½ cup chunk-style peanut butter*

*1 egg yolk*

*1 ½ tablespoons milk*

*1 teaspoon vanilla extract*

FILLING

*About ⅓ cup firm Concord grape jam, preferably made without added pectin, or any firm berry jam*

**1.** *Make the cookie dough:* Sift together into a mixing bowl the flour, sugar, baking soda, and salt. Add the butter and peanut butter and, using a pastry blender or two knives criss-crossed scissors-fashion (or in the food processor, flicking the motor on and off rapidly), cut them into the dry ingredients until the mixture is like coarse meal.

**2.** In a small bowl, beat the egg yolk with the milk and vanilla. Stir the egg mixture into the first mixture to make a dough. Divide the dough in half, form the halves into balls, wrap them, and refrigerate for about 1 hour, or until the dough is well chilled.

**3.** Preheat the oven to 350°F, with an oven rack in the center position. Lightly grease one or two baking sheets.

**4.** Roll out one portion of the chilled dough between sheets of plastic wrap until it is ⅛ inch thick. Lift off the upper sheet of plastic wrap and cut the dough into rounds with a 2½-inch cookie or biscuit cutter. Lift the rounds onto the prepared baking sheet, placing them at least 1½ inches apart. Gather and reroll the scraps and cut more rounds until all the dough has been used; you should have 18.

**5.** *Add the filling:* Spoon a rounded half teaspoon (use a measuring spoon) of grape jam into the center of each round.

**6.** Roll out the second portion of dough and cut more rounds as in step 4 above. Lay a round over the filling of each cookie, then gather the scraps and make more rounds until each cookie has an upper crust. With the tines of a table fork, crimp the layers together all around the edge. (You may also prick the tops of each cookie once or twice.)

**7.** Bake the cookies, one sheet at a time, in the center of the preheated oven for about 12 to 13 minutes, or until they are firm and only lightly browned; they should not be overbaked. Cool the cookies on the baking sheet for 5 minutes, then lift them onto wire racks to cool completely.

**8.** The cookies may be stored in a tightly covered container at room temperature for a few days, or they may be refrigerated for up to two weeks.

*Makes about 18 2¾-inch pies*

# RAISIN PIE COOKIES

Stuffed with raisins aromatized with sherry and lemon, these little pies are a mellow mouthful, especially welcome as an accompaniment for coffee. Kids tend to take theirs straight—or with a milk chaser.

COOKIE DOUGH

¼ cup (½ stick) unsalted butter or margarine, at room temperature

2 tablespoons vegetable shortening

½ cup granulated sugar

1 egg

1 egg yolk

1 teaspoon finely grated lemon rind (colored outer layer only, no pith)

Big pinch of ground nutmeg

1¾ cups all-purpose flour

1 teaspoon baking powder

¼ teaspoon salt

Lemon juice, if needed

FILLING

¾ cup dark raisins, coarsely chopped

¼ cup plus 2 tablespoons (packed) light brown sugar

2 tablespoons sherry (any kind), or substitute orange juice

½ teaspoon finely grated lemon rind (colored outer layer only, no pith)

1 tablespoon all-purpose flour

2 tablespoons water

1 teaspoon vanilla extract

1. *Make the cookie dough:* In a mixing bowl (using a wooden spoon) or in the large bowl of an electric mixer, cream the butter and vegetable shortening together until soft, then beat in the sugar to make a fluffy mixture. Beat in the

egg, egg yolk, 1 teaspoon lemon rind, and nutmeg.

**2.** Sift together the flour, baking powder, and salt. Stir the flour mixture into the creamed mixture. The resulting dough should be crumbly, but it should be moist enough to hold together when a sample is squeezed lightly. If the dough is too dry, mix in a few drops of lemon juice, but don't overdo it.

**3.** Divide the dough in half; form each half into a ball. Wrap the balls in plastic wrap and chill them thoroughly, about 1 hour. Meanwhile, prepare the filling.

**4.** *Make the filling:* In a small saucepan, combine the raisins, sugar, sherry, and lemon rind. Stir the flour and water together until smooth, then stir the mixture thoroughly into the raisin mixture. Bring the filling to a boil over medium heat, stirring, and cook it until thickened, stirring constantly. Add the vanilla and set the filling aside to cool.

**5.** *Shape and fill the cookies:* Preheat the oven to 350°F, with an oven rack in the center position. Lightly grease one or two baking sheets.

**6.** Roll one portion of the chilled dough out ⅛ inch thick between two sheets of plastic wrap. Lift off the upper sheet of plastic and cut the dough into rounds with a 2½-inch cookie or biscuit cutter. Lift the rounds onto a prepared baking sheet, placing them at least 1½ inches apart. Gather and reroll the scraps and cut more rounds until the portion of dough has been used.

**7.** Stir the cooled filling again and place about a level measuring teaspoonful in the center of each round. (You can use a little more, but there's a slight risk of leakage as the cookies bake.)

**8.** Roll out and cut the other portion of chilled dough as described in step 6 above. Lay a round over the filling of each cookie, then gather the scraps and make more rounds until every cookie has an upper crust. With the tines of a table fork, crimp the layers together all around the edge. Prick the top of each cookie once or twice.

**9.** Bake the cookies, one sheet at a time, in the center of the preheated oven for about 11 to 13 minutes, or until they are firm and golden, with golden brown edges. Cool the cookies on the baking sheet for a few minutes, then cool them completely on wire racks.

**10.** Store the cookies in a covered container at room temperature for a day or two, or refrigerate them for up to two weeks. They freeze well, too.

***Makes*** *about 18 3-inch cookies*

# DATE AND NUT HALF-MOON PIES

**M**ooning about with dates, walnuts, and the same crust used for the Overstuffed Cranberry, Nut and Orange Cookies on page 118 and the Raisin Pie Cookies on page 114 resulted in these tender crescents. Few kitchens possess a round cutter large enough for shaping them, but a clean, dry 7-ounce tuna can, both ends removed, is a dandy makeshift. A standard (2½-inch) cutter can be used, but the cookies will be trickier to shape.

### COOKIE DOUGH

¼ cup (½ stick) unsalted butter, at room temperature

2 tablespoons vegetable shortening

½ cup granulated sugar

1 egg

1 egg yolk

1 teaspoon finely grated lemon rind (colored outer layer only, no pith)

Big pinch (⅛ teaspoon) ground nutmeg

1¾ cups all-purpose flour

1 teaspoon baking powder

¼ teaspoon salt

Lemon juice, if needed

### FILLING

1 cup (packed) packaged pitted dates, whole or cut up (they come in both forms)

½ cup water

2 tablespoons honey, or substitute dark or light corn syrup

½ cup coarsely chopped walnuts

1½ to 3 teaspoons lemon juice, as needed

**1.** *Make the dough:* In a mixing bowl (using a wooden spoon) or in the large bowl of an electric mixer, cream the butter and vegetable shortening together until soft, then beat in the sugar to make a fluffy mixture. Beat in the egg, egg yolk, lemon rind, and nutmeg.

**2.** Sift together the flour, baking powder, and salt. Stir the flour mixture into the creamed mixture. The resulting dough should be crumbly, but it should hold together when a sample is squeezed lightly. If the dough is too dry to hold together, mix in a few drops of lemon juice, but don't overdo it—the dough should not be moist.

**3.** Divide the dough in half; form each half into a ball. Wrap the balls of dough and chill them thoroughly, 1 hour or more. Meanwhile, prepare the filling.

**4.** *Make the filling:* Chop the dates coarsely, or snip them with scissors, dipped frequently in water. Combine the dates in a saucepan with the water and honey or corn syrup. Bring the mixture to a boil over medium heat and cook, stirring, for 3 to 5 minutes, until it is thick. Remove the filling from the heat and add the nuts and lemon juice to taste, 1½ teaspoons or more. Cool the filling.

**5.** *Shape and fill the cookies:* Preheat the oven to 350°F, with an oven rack in the center position. Lightly grease one or two baking sheets.

**6.** Roll out one portion of dough between sheets of plastic wrap until it is ⅛ inch thick. Lift off the upper sheet of plastic and, using a 3¼- or 3½-inch cutter (lacking one this size, use a clean, dry 7-ounce tuna can with both ends removed), cut the dough into rounds. Spoon a rounded measuring teaspoonful of filling slightly to one side of the center of each round. Fold the pastry over to make a half-moon and crimp the curved edges together with the tines of a fork. Place the pies on a prepared baking sheet, spacing them about 1½ inches apart. Gather and reroll the scraps to make more cookies.

**7.** Bake the cookies, one sheet at a time, in the center of the preheated oven for 12 to 15 minutes, or until they are firm and the edges are golden brown. Lift the pies onto a wire rack to cool completely, then store them at room temperature (for a day or two) in a covered container; or refrigerate them for up to two weeks or freeze them for longer storage.

*Makes 20 to 22 3½-inch crescent cookies*

# OVERSTUFFED CRANBERRY, NUT AND ORANGE COOKIES

They're not for wintertime only, these little pies filled with a subtle, quickly cooked mixture of cranberries, walnuts, and a touch of orange peel; you can make them at any moment of cookie-hunger, using canned cranberry sauce. But the cranberry sauce should be a good brand—a bargain sauce may be watery and/or lacking in flavor.

COOKIE DOUGH

¼ cup (½ stick) unsalted butter or margarine, at room temperature

2 tablespoons vegetable shortening

½ cup granulated sugar

1 egg

1 egg yolk

½ teaspoon vanilla extract

1 teaspoon finely grated orange rind (colored outer layer only, no pith)

1¾ cups all-purpose flour

1 teaspoon baking powder

¼ teaspoon salt

Orange juice, if needed

FILLING

⅔ cup whole-berry cranberry sauce, homemade or canned

⅓ cup coarsely chopped walnuts

1½ teaspoons finely grated orange rind (colored outer layer only, no pith)

1 tablespoon granulated sugar

1½ teaspoons all-purpose flour

**1.** *Make the dough:* In a mixing bowl (using a wooden spoon) or in the large bowl of an electric mixer, cream the butter (or margarine) and vegetable shortening together until soft, then beat in the sugar to make a fluffy mixture. Beat in the egg, egg yolk, vanilla, and grated orange rind.

**2.** Sift together the flour, baking powder, and salt. Stir the flour mixture into the creamed mixture to make a crumbly dough that holds together when a sample is squeezed lightly. If the dough is too dry to hold together in this fashion, lightly mix in a teaspoonful of orange juice and test the dough again. Add a few more drops of orange juice, if necessary (this will depend on the moisture content of the flour), but don't make the dough too moist, or it will be difficult to handle.

**3.** Divide the dough in half; form each half into a ball. Wrap the balls in plastic wrap and chill them thoroughly, about 1 hour. Meanwhile, prepare the filling.

**4.** *Make the filling:* In a small saucepan, combine the cranberry sauce, walnuts, and orange rind. Stir the sugar and flour together, then add them to the cranberry mixture. Bring the filling to a boil over medium heat, stirring, and cook it for a moment or two until it has thickened. Set the filling aside to cool completely.

**5.** *Shape and fill the cookies:* Preheat the oven to 350°F, with an oven rack in the center position. Lightly grease one or two baking sheets.

**6.** Roll one portion of the dough out to ⅛-inch thickness between two sheets of plastic wrap. Lift off the upper sheet of plastic wrap and cut the dough into rounds with a 2½-inch cookie or biscuit cutter. Lift the rounds onto a prepared baking sheet, placing them at least 1½ inches apart. Gather and reroll the scraps and cut more rounds until all the first portion of dough has been used.

**7.** Stir the cooled filling and place about a level measuring teaspoonful in the center of each round.

**8.** Roll out and cut the second portion of chilled dough as described in step 6. Lay a round over the filling of each cookie, then gather the scraps and make more rounds until every cookie has an upper crust. With the tines of a table fork, crimp the layers together all around the edge of each cookie and prick the top once or twice.

**9.** Bake the cookies, one sheet at a time, in the center of the preheated oven for 11 to 13 minutes, or until they are firm, golden on top, and golden brown around the edges. Cool the cookies on the baking sheet for a few minutes until firm, then cool them completely on wire racks.

**10.** Store the cookies in a closed container at room temperature for a day or two, or refrigerate them for longer storage, up to two weeks. They also freeze well.

***Makes*** *about 18 3-inch cookies*

# FRUIT NEWTS

**F**ill these tender, not-too-sweet bars with figs and raisins, or prunes and walnuts, or apricots and almonds—recipes for all three fillings are given. Any one of the three newts is tempting enough to bring on chain consumption, especially by those who grew up regarding the store-bought version as a great treat. Eat your heart out, makers of trademarked and shelf-dwelling Fig Newtons—these are better. (Does anyone know where ''Newton'' came from?)

## FIG AND RAISIN FRUIT NEWTS

COOKIE DOUGH

6 tablespoons (¾ stick) unsalted butter, at room temperature

⅓ cup (packed) light brown sugar

⅓ cup granulated sugar

2 eggs

¼ teaspoon lemon extract (or substitute 1 teaspoon very finely grated lemon rind, colored outer layer only, no pith)

1 teaspoon vanilla extract

1 cup plus 2 tablespoons all-purpose flour

1 cup whole-wheat flour (or substitute additional all-purpose flour)

2 tablespoons cornmeal, preferably stone ground

½ teaspoon salt

¼ teaspoon baking soda

FIG AND RAISIN FILLING

1½ cups coarsely chopped stemmed dried figs, preferably light in color

½ cup coarsely chopped dark or light raisins

2 cups water

1 tablespoon grated orange rind (colored outer layer only, no pith)

⅓ cup granulated sugar

½ teaspoon vanilla extract

**1.** *Make the cookie dough:* In a mixing bowl (using a wooden spoon) or in the large bowl of an electric mixer, cream the butter until soft. Beat in the brown sugar, granulated sugar, and the eggs, beating until the mixture is thoroughly combined. Stir in the lemon extract (or grated rind) and vanilla.

**2.** Sift together the two flours, cornmeal, salt, and baking soda. Stir the flour mixture thoroughly into the creamed mixture. Form the dough into a ball and wrap it in plastic wrap. Refrigerate the dough until it is well chilled, at least an hour, preferably two or three.

**3.** *Make the filling:* In a saucepan, combine the figs, raisins, water, and orange rind. Bring them to a boil over medium heat, then lower the heat and simmer the fruit, uncovered, until it is tender, 15 minutes or more (depending on the initial texture of the fruit). Check frequently; when the fruit is done, the water should have been absorbed. However, if the mixture seems dry before that point, add a little more water.

**4.** Chop the mixture briefly in a blender or food processor, just until it is finely chopped—don't let it become pasty. Return the fruit to the saucepan, add the sugar, and cook the mixture again, stirring, for about 5 minutes, until it is quite thick. Add the vanilla and let the filling cool.

**5.** Preheat the oven to 350°F, with an oven rack in the center position. Lightly grease one or two baking sheets.

**6.** Divide the chilled dough in half; return one half to the refrigerator. Roll out the other portion of dough between two sheets of plastic wrap until it measures slightly over 9 x 10 inches. Uncover the dough and, using a ruler or straight edge, trim it into a neat rectangle 9 inches wide and 10 inches long. Break up the trimmings, scatter the pieces over the dough, re-cover it, and roll it again briefly to incorporate the extra bits, being sure to keep the edges straight. (It doesn't matter if the piece grows slightly in size.) Cut the dough into two lengthwise strips.

**7.** Spoon ½ cup of the filling down the center of each strip, then shape it into an even, narrow line with the back of the spoon. Fold one side of the dough, then the other, over the filling to make a tube; press the seam lightly. Place the roll, seam down, on the prepared cookie sheet and form it into an even shape. Repeat, making another roll with the second half of the dough and another ½ cup of filling. Place the second roll at least 3 inches away from the first one on the baking sheet.

**8.** Make two more rolls, as in steps 6 and 7 above, and place them on the second baking sheet, using the remaining chilled dough and remaining filling. (If you have only one baking sheet, delay this step until it has cooled completely after baking the first two rolls.)

**9.** Bake the rolls, one sheet at a time, in the center of the preheated oven for about 20 minutes, until they are firm and golden brown. Let them cool on the baking sheet for 5 minutes, or until they have firmed up slightly, then lift them carefully onto a wire rack to cool completely.

**10.** Trim off the ends of the rolls (a tasty snack) and cut the rolls on a slight slant into 1-inch bars. Store the cookies in an airtight container at room temperature for a few days, or refrigerate them for longer keeping. They freeze well, too.

***Makes** about 40 bars, 1 x 2½ inches*

## PRUNE AND WALNUT FRUIT NEWTS

COOKIE DOUGH

*Dough for Fig and Raisin Fruit Newts,
    page 120*

FILLING

*2 cups pitted tender prunes, quartered*

*2 cups water*

*½ cup coarsely chopped walnuts*

*⅓ cup granulated sugar*

*1 teaspoon or more lemon juice, as
    needed*

**1.** Make the cookie dough and chill it as directed in steps 1 and 2 of the recipe for Fig and Raisin Fruit Newts.

**2.** *Make the filling:* In a saucepan, combine the prunes and the water. Bring them to a boil over medium heat, then lower the heat and simmer the prunes, uncovered, about 20 minutes, or until they are quite tender. If there is a great deal of liquid (there should be just enough to cover the bottom of the pan), cook the prunes a little longer to incorporate it, watching to prevent sticking.

Chop the prunes to a fine texture, using a food processor, a blender, or a food mill. Return the fruit to the saucepan. Add the walnuts and sugar and cook the mixture, stirring constantly, until it is thick enough to mound up in a spoon, a matter of a couple of minutes. Add the lemon juice and cool the filling.

**3.** Roll the dough, fill and bake the rolls, and slice and store the bars as directed in steps 5 through 10 of the preceding recipe.

*Makes about 40 bars, 1 x 2½ inches*

## APRICOT AND ALMOND FRUIT NEWTS

COOKIE DOUGH

*Dough for Fig and Raisin Fruit Newts, page 120*

FILLING

*1½ cups (lightly packed) high-quality dried apricots, quartered*
*2 cups water*
*1 teaspoon grated lemon rind (colored outer layer only, no pith)*
*½ cup coarsely chopped blanched almonds*
*½ cup granulated sugar*
*6 to 10 drops almond extract*

**1.** Make the cookie dough and chill it as directed in steps 1 and 2 of the recipe for Fig and Raisin Fruit Newts.

**2.** *Make the filling:* In a saucepan, combine the dried apricots, water, and lemon rind. Let them stand for 20 minutes. Set the pan over medium heat, bring the fruit to a boil, then lower the heat and simmer for 15 to 20 minutes, until most of the water has been absorbed. (The apricots will remain rather firm.) Chop the apricots to a fine texture in a food processor, blender, or food mill. Return the fruit to the saucepan. Add the almonds and sugar and cook the filling again, stirring constantly for a few minutes, until it is thick enough to mound up in a spoon. Cool the filling. Add drops of almond flavoring carefully, stirring and tasting after the first 6 drops; don't overdo the flavoring, which is powerful. Add more sugar, if needed; the filling should be a cross between tart and sweet.

**3.** Roll the dough, fill and bake the rolls, and slice and store the bars as described in steps 5 through 10 of the recipe for Fig and Raisin Fruit Newts.

*Makes about 40 bars, 1 x 2½ inches*

# LEMON PIEFACES

With an intensely lemony filling, its tartness smoothed by butter, these little pies are made with a tender crust that can also be baked as plain flat cookies (just roll, cut, sprinkle with coarse sugar, and bake). Any leftover filling will keep for up to three weeks in the refrigerator; it's a delicious spread for toast.

LEMON FILLING (makes 2 cups)

*½ cup (1 stick) unsalted butter, cut up*

*1½ cups granulated sugar*

*⅓ cup strained fresh lemon juice (juice of 2 to 3 lemons)*

*1½ tablespoons very finely chopped or grated fresh lemon rind (colored outer layer only, no pith)*

*Pinch of salt*

*3 eggs*

*1 egg yolk*

COOKIE DOUGH

*1 cup (2 sticks) unsalted butter, at room temperature*

*1 cup confectioners' (10X) sugar, sifted*

*2 egg yolks*

*1 teaspoon vanilla extract*

*3 cups all-purpose flour*

*½ cup cornstarch*

*½ teaspoon salt*

*2 to 4 teaspoons strained fresh lemon juice, as needed*

GARNISH (optional)

*Thin curls of lemon or orange peel*

**1.** *Make the lemon filling:* In the top section of a double boiler or in a very heavy saucepan, combine the butter, sugar, lemon juice, lemon rind, and salt. Set the double boiler top or the saucepan over very low heat and stir the mixture constantly until the butter has melted and the sugar has dissolved.

**2.** In a small bowl, beat the eggs and the egg yolk together until they are well mixed. Stirring the warm butter mixture constantly, strain the eggs into it. Set the double boiler top over simmering water or return the saucepan to low heat and cook the filling, stirring or whisking it constantly, until the mixture thickens enough to coat a spoon heavily and becomes glossy. Immediately scrape the filling into a bowl and cover its surface with a piece of plastic wrap, smoothed down. Cool the filling, then refrigerate it until it is needed.

**3.** *Make the cookie dough:* Preheat the oven to 375°F, with an oven rack in the center position. Cut a 12 x 16–inch sheet of aluminum foil into 12 squares measuring 4 x 4 inches each. Set them aside.

**4.** In a mixing bowl (using a wooden spoon) or in the large bowl of an electric mixer, cream the butter until soft. Beat in the confectioners' sugar until fluffy. Beat in the egg yolks and the vanilla, mixing well.

**5.** Sift together the flour, cornstarch, and salt. Add the flour mixture to the creamed mixture and stir them together thoroughly. While mixing, add 2 teaspoons of the lemon juice. If the dough proves to be too crumbly to hold together when pressed lightly, add up to 2 teaspoons more lemon juice, mixing it in a few drops at a time. Form the dough into a ball, then divide it into four equal portions. Cover three of them with plastic while you shape the first dozen pielets.

**6.** Roll out one portion of the dough ⅛ inch thick between two sheets of plastic wrap. Peel off the upper sheet and cut the dough into rounds with a 2¾-inch cookie cutter, preferably one with a fluted edge. Then gather the scraps and reroll them between the sheets of plastic wrap to make more shells. Repeat with the remaining portions of dough; each portion of dough will make 12 little pies.

**7.** *To shape pie-shell cookies:* Place a round of dough in the center of a foil square. Dip the base of a small jar (spice jar size, 1½ inches in diameter) into flour and set it carefully in the center of the pastry. Upend the whole business in one hand and with the other press the foil and pastry gently over the bottom and up the sides of the jar—don't squeeze, just press lightly. Press the foil extending above the pastry closely to the jar. Turn everything over again, re-move the shell from the jar, and set the shell, in its mold, on a baking sheet. Adjust the shell, if necessary, to sit flat, with evenly turned-up edges. Repeat, placing the shells about 2 inches apart, until all the dough has been used. (This is quicker to do than to describe.)

**8.** *Fill the shells:* Measure ½ teaspoon of the lemon filling into each shell, reserving the rest for later. Bake the partially filled pie cookies in the preheated oven for 12 to 14 minutes, until the pastry is firm and golden brown. Remove the foil-enclosed shells to a wire rack and let them cool.

**9.** Remove the foil from the shells (you can reserve the foil squares for another batch of cookies). Spoon from ½ to 1 teaspoon of additional filling into each shell and serve the cookies within a few hours. (Reserve some of the partly filled shells to be filled and served later, if you like. They should be refrigerated, together with the remaining filling.)

**10.** For a festive garnish, the little pies may be topped with a thin curl of lemon or orange peel. Don't worry about their keeping qualities if you have some filled pies on hand; refrigerated, they become mellower in texture as the crisp shell softens, but they will be fine eating for up to three days.

*Makes 4 dozen 2-inch pies*

# INDEX*

*All cookies are listed by name in
the contents.